JUST ADD KIDS

Ring 'Round Jericho

and 50 Other Bible Games for Preschoolers

Abingdon Press
Nashville

Just Add Kids: Ring 'Round Jericho and 50 other Bible Games for Preschoolers

Copyright © 2000 Abingdon Press

All rights reserved.

No part of this work, EXCEPT PATTERNS AND PAGES COVERED BY THE FOLLOWING NOTICE, may be reproduced or transmitted in any form or by any means, electronic or mechanical, including photocopying and recording, or by any information storage or retrieval system, except as may be expressly permitted by the 1976 Copyright Act or in writing from the publisher. Requests for permission should be addressed in writing to Abingdon Press, 201 Eighth Avenue South, Nashville, TN 37203.

ISBN 0-687-04820-6

Unless otherwise noted, Scripture quotations are from the New Revised Standard Version of the Bible. Copyright © 1989 by the Division of Christian Education of the National Council of the Churches of Christ in the United States of America. Used by permission. All rights reserved.

Scripture quotations identified as *Good News Bible* are from the *Good News Bible: The Bible in Today's English Version*. Old Testament: Copyright © American Bible Society 1976, 1992; New Testament: Copyright © American Bible Society 1966, 1971, 1976, 1992. Used by permission.

The purchaser of this book is entitled to reproduce ANY PATTERN, provided the copyright notice is included.

Lead Editor: Daphna Flegal
Editor: Betsi H. Smith
Contributing Writer: Sharilyn S. Adair
Designed by: Paige Easter
Illustrated by: Robert S. Jones
Cover Photographs: Ron Benedict

00 01 02 03 04 05 06 07 08 09—10 9 8 7 6 5 4 3 2 1

MANUFACTURED IN THE UNITED STATES OF AMERICA

Preschool Games
Table of Contents

5 Introduction
6 Using Games to Teach God's Word

7 Old Testament

8 **Sun, Moon, Stars** (Lights Turnover • Sun Tag)
9 **God Made Animals** (What Flies? • Sheep Chase • Where's the Mouse?)
12 **In God's Image** (Stand Up, Sit Down • True or False?)
13 **Noah** (Two by Two)
14 **Abraham and Sarah**
(Caravan Capers • Walk Like a Camel • The Laughing Game)
17 **Jacob's Dream** (Harump, Harump • Angel Antics)
19 **Joseph and His Brothers** (Joseph, Joseph)
21 **Baby Moses** (Name Names)
23 **The Burning Bush** (Jump!)
25 **Let My People Go!** (Ribbit, Ribbit, Bzzz! • Croak 'n Creep)
27 **The Red Sea** (Red Sea Run • Jump Over the Sea)
28 **In the Wilderness** (Run, Quail, Run • Picture Turnover)
31 **The Ten Commandments** (At-TEN-tion! • Commandment Hop)
33 **Joshua and the Walls of Jericho** (Ring 'Round Jericho)
34 **Serve the Lord** (Number One)
36 **Ruth and Naomi** (Pass-It Basket • Which Comes First? • Kindness Capers)
40 **Hannah** (Steppin' Out • Hannah's Hop • Growing With God)
42 **Samuel's Calling** (Listen 'n Do)
43 **Samuel Finds David**
(Choosin' and Movin' • David's Dance • Hearts 'n Hands)
46 **David and Jonathan** (Friendship Feats • Friendship Follies)
48 **Solomon's Temple** (Temple Marching • King Solomon Says • Royal Procession)
51 **Esther** (Royal Romp • Queen Esther, Queen Esther)
52 **Jeremiah** (Jeremiah Jump • Big Ball Bop)
53 **Potters** (Pottery Match • To Market, To Market)
55 **Jonah** (Jonah-in-the-Fish • Obey Simon • Yes!)

57 New Testament

- 58 **The Wise Men** (Gift Exchange • Star Stretch)
- 61 **The Beatitudes**
  (Happy Faces, Happy Hearts • Happy Hands • Happy Hero Hop)
- 65 **The Least of These** (Birds Fly Like This)
- 66 **The Lost Sheep** (Sheep Search • Yes! • Fuzzy Wuzzy Was a . . .)
- 68 **Forgive One Another**
  (Cat and Mouse • Feelings Follies • Smile! Jesus Loves . . .)
- 70 **The Withered Hand** (Glove Grab • Handy Work • Handtalk Zoo)
- 74 **Two by Two** (Traveling Twofers • Traffic Light Tiptoe)
- 77 **Jesus and the Children**
  (Through the Crowd • Wave and Wiggle • Stop!)
- 80 **Jesus' Birth** (Follow the Leader • Praise Ways • Ring Around the Baby)
- 82 **Jesus Grows** (Wonder Works • Learning Limbo • Hoppy Talk)
- 84 **The Messiah** (Tell the Truth)
- 85 **Jesus Calls Fishermen**
  (Disciple Doings • Bible-Times Play • Bring a Friend)
- 87 **The Prodigal Son** (This Little Piggy)
- 89 **The Ten Lepers** (Sign of the Times • Ten Hop! • Comeback Kid)
- 91 **Zacchaeus** (Jump Up • Where's Zacchaeus?)
- 93 **Jesus' Baptism** (In and Out the River • Fly Away • Water Wiggles)
- 95 **Mud in the Eye** (Color Hop • I Spy • Noisy Nonsense)
- 97 **Foot Washing** (Feet Fun)
- 98 **Pentecost** (Wind Whipper)
- 99 **Peter and John Heal the Man at the Gate**
  (Leaping Feet • Shake a Leg)
- 101 **Dorcas** (Guess What Dorcas Made • Tunic Tiptoe • In and Out)
- 103 **Peter and Cornelius** (Down the Street • Peter, Peter)
- 105 **Paul's Travels** (Travel With Paul)
- 106 **Paul and Silas in Jail** (Stuck in Jail • Jailhouse Shake)
- 108 **Paul's Letters** (Love in Action • Lub Dub Rub)
- 109 **Fruits of the Spirit** (Thank-You Pass • Kindness Capers)

- 111 Index by Bible Reference
- 112 Index by Subject

Introduction
Welcome to Just Add Kids

As you look out across your classroom, you see one child yawning, another child trying to climb a bookshelf, and two others in a shoving match. What will you do with them? Maybe it's time to play a game.

Ring 'Round Jericho and 50 Other Bible Games for Preschoolers is loaded with games that will cure your classroom blahs. Some use reproducible pages, which are included here. And since each game in *Ring 'Round Jericho* relates to a specific event in the Bible, your children are learning while they're playing.

Each child in your class is unique, with his or her own family background and experiences. But preschoolers do have some common traits. Understanding those traits will help you in your classroom:

- Preschoolers have lots of energy. They enjoy movement, although they are still struggling with fine motor skills.
- Preschoolers love anything silly, whether they're laughing, saying nonsense words, or singing a fun song. They are learning to identify colors and shapes.
- Preschoolers are just beginning to share. They are learning to interact, to respect others' feelings, and to wait until it's their turn. They may have a hard time leaving their parents.

For guidelines on how to make the most out of your game time, see the article on the next page. For other resources that will help you make your class time the best that it can be, don't miss the other books in the *Just Add Kids* collection:

- *Don't Get Wet Feet and 50 Other Bible Stories for Preschoolers.*
- *Footprints on the Wall and 50 Other Bible Crafts for Preschoolers.*
- *The Jailhouse Rocked and 50 Other Bible Stories for Elementary Children.*
- *Downright Upright and 50 Other Bible Games for Elementary Children.*
- *From Bags to Bushes and 50 Other Bible Crafts for Elementary Children.*

Using Games to Teach God's Word

Children learn through movement. As they hop, stretch, race, and parade, they are grasping the principles that each particular game is designed to teach. Games also provide a welcome break from the classroom routine. They give children a chance to fellowship and to have fun together. And for those children who don't excel at reading or crafts, game time may be the only time some children feel they are doing something well.

Follow these simple guidelines to make game time fun, safe, and successful.

- **Plan ahead.** Decide where the game will be played in your classroom, and clear the space ahead of time. Make any signs, props, or game cards you will be using. Practice the game yourself, to make sure you understand exactly how it should be played.

- **Balance activities.** Choose where game time will fall in your lesson plan. You might not want to play an active game just before you want the children to sit quietly for your worship time. But games can work well after the children have been sitting for a while.

- **Put safety first.** Clear the area of hazards. Check for slippery floors; if you've just finished a messy craft, look for spills on the floor. Remove any rugs that can move or trip a child. Move furniture out of the way. Make sure there are no sharp edges on tables or counter tops. If the game involves a ball, caution the children to never throw a ball at someone's face.

- **Be aware of disabilities.** If a child in your classroom has a physical or mental disability, use games that will let that child participate on an equal footing with the others. If the child has a mobility problem, avoid or adapt games that involve running. If the child has a learning disability, avoid or adapt games that involve putting letters in order.

- **Play cooperatively.** Whenever possible, remove the element of competition from the games you play. Encourage the children to clap for everyone. Find something positive to say about each child, not just the fastest or the smartest. If you are giving out prizes, give them to everyone. Say, for example: "You all played the game so well, I want everyone to have a sticker." Having fun should be more important than winning.

OLD TESTAMENT

Sun, Moon, Stars

Game 1

Lights Turnover

Play a game with the children similar to "Fruit Basket Turnover." Have the children stand in a circle. Tell each child that he or she is either a sun, a moon, or a star. Have the child repeat what she or he is pretending to be.

Say: God made the sun, moon, and stars. God planned for the sun to shine during the day and the moon and the stars to shine during the night. Let's play a game. When I say, "God made the stars," everyone pretending to be a star change places in the circle. When I say, "God made the sun," everyone pretending to be a sun change places. When I say, "God made the moon," everyone pretending to be a moon change places. When I say, "Lights turnover," everyone change places.

Play the game as long as the children show interest.

Say: The Bible tells us that when God made the sun, moon, and stars, God saw that it was good.

© 1999 Abingdon Press.

Game 2

Sun Tag

Have the children move to an open area of the room.

Say: Let's pretend that you are stars and I am the sun. It is night, and all the stars are twinkling in the sky.

Have the children move about the room as stars.

Say: Now it's almost morning. Here comes the sun. When the sun is shining, no one can see the stars twinkling in the sky. If the sun tags you, crouch down and be very still.

Pretend to be the sun and tag each child. When a child is tagged, have her or him crouch down and be still. Play until all the children have been tagged.

Say: We thank God for the sun, moon, and stars.

© 1999 Abingdon Press.

Bible
Genesis 1:14-18

God Made Animals

Game 1

What Flies?

Have the children stand in a circle.

Say: Let's play a game that is played at children's parties in a country named Germany. The game is called "Ducks Fly." When I name something that really flies, flap your arms like wings. When I name something that does not fly, keep your arms still.

Call out:

Ducks fly. (*Flap arms.*)
Dogs fly. (*Hold arms still.*)
Redbirds fly. (*Flap arms.*)
Butterflies fly. (*Flap arms.*)
Bumblebees fly. (*Flap arms.*)
Houses fly. (*Hold arms still.*)
Bluebirds fly. (*Flap arms.*)
Fireflies fly. (*Flap arms.*)
Cats fly. (*Hold arms still.*)

© 1998 Abingdon Press.

Bible
Genesis
1:20-25

Game 2

Sheep Chase

Say: Let's play a game children play in a country called Egypt. To play the game, let's pretend that we are sheep.

Have the children move to an open area of the room and stand in a circle. Choose one child to be in the middle. This child is the wolf. Have the children shout: "Wolf, wolf, what are you doing?" Have the wolf answer, "I'm sleeping."

Have the children keep shouting at the wolf. Then have the wolf shout, "I'm chasing you!" Have the wolf chase after the sheep. The first sheep caught is the next wolf.

© 1998 Abingdon Press.

Game 3

Supplies: mouse (see page 11), scissors, tape or glue

Where's the Mouse?

Photocopy and cut out the mouse (see page 11). Tape or glue the mouse together as pictured on the page. Have the children move to an open area of the room.

Say: God made all the animals. God made great big animals like elephants. (*Have the children pretend to be elephants.*) God made smaller animals like cats. (*Have the children pretend to be cats.*) And God made tiny animals like mice. (*Have the children pretend to be mice.*)

Have the children sit down on the floor. Show the children the paper mouse.

Say: Let's pretend that we are cats. While all the cats are sleeping, I will hide the mouse somewhere in the room. When I say, "Squeak! Squeak!" the cats can wake up and start looking for the mouse.

Have the children pretend to take a cat nap and to close their eyes while you hide the mouse somewhere in the room. Then let the cats look all around until someone finds the mouse. Play the game several times.

© 1999 Abingdon Press.

GLUE TAIL HERE

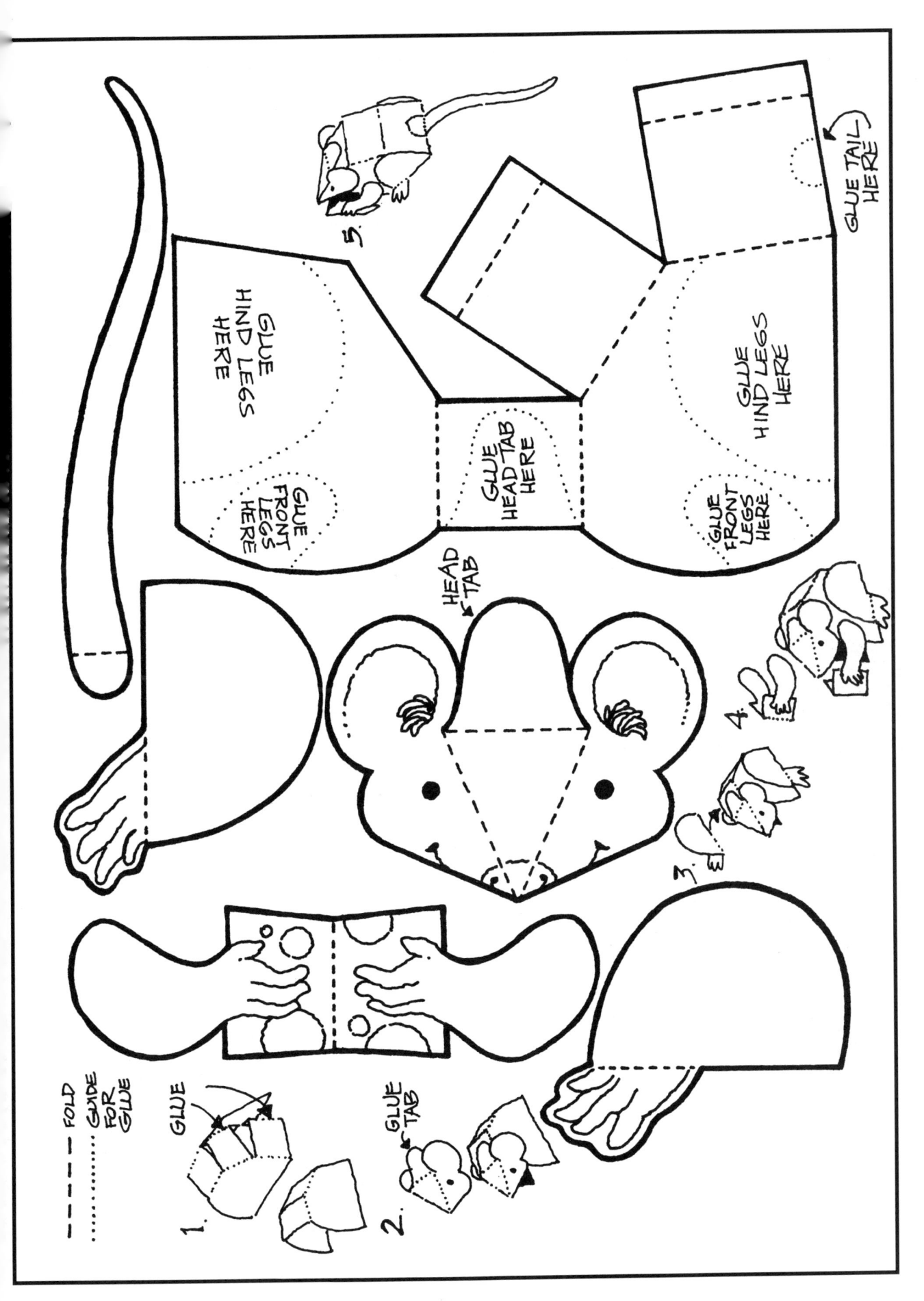

GLUE HIND LEGS HERE

GLUE HEAD TAB HERE

GLUE FRONT LEGS HERE

GLUE HIND LEGS HERE

GLUE FRONT LEGS HERE

5.

HEAD TAB

4.

3.

1. GLUE

2. GLUE TAB

- - - FOLD
· · · GUIDE FOR GLUE

Permission granted to photocopy for local church use. © 1999 Abingdon Press.

11

In God's Image

Game 1

Stand Up, Sit Down

Have the children sit down.

Say: God made people with brown hair. If you have brown hair, stand up. (*Have the children with brown hair stand up.*) Sit down. God made people with blonde hair. If you have blonde hair, stand up. (*Have the children with blonde hair stand up.*) Sit down.

Continue naming hair color, eye color, and other physical characteristics until every child has stood up.

Say: If God made you, stand up! Sit down! Shout, shout, shout! (*Have the children shout, "Hooray!"*)

© 1999 Abingdon Press.

Game 2

True or False?

Make the following statements about God's world. If the statement is true, have the children nod their heads yes and say, "Yes! God's world is good!" If the statement is false, have the children shake their heads no and say, "No! Not in God's world!"

God made clouds to float up in the sky.
(*Yes! God's world is good!*)
God made great big whales to swim in the sea.
(*Yes! God's world is good!*)
God made cats to bark, "Woof, woof!"
(*No! Not in God's world!*)
God made dogs to bark, "Woof, woof!"
(*Yes! God's world is good!*)

© 1999 Abingdon Press.

Bible
Genesis 1:26-27

Noah

Game

Two by Two

Have the children move to an open area of the room.

Say:
Two by two,
Two by two,
Let's all be animals
Two by two.
Let's be (*name an animal*).

Have the children pretend to move like that animal. Repeat the refrain several times, changing the last line to name a different animal each time.

Ask: What is your favorite animal?

Repeat the refrain again, ending with, "Let's be our favorite animal."

Encourage the children to move like their favorite animals. As the children are moving, touch the children on the shoulder two at a time. Tell the children to pretend that they are animals going into the ark.

Say: God told Noah to bring his family and two of every animal on the boat. Noah and his family trusted God to take care of them on the boat.

© 1997 Abingdon Press.

Bible
Genesis
6:14-19

Abraham and Sarah

Game 1

Supplies: camel mask (see page 16), scissors, tape, drinking straws, crayons or markers

Caravan Capers

Before class begins, photocopy and use scissors to cut out a camel mask (see page 16) for each child. Cut out the holes for the eyes and two slits along one edge. Give each child a mask and a drinking straw. Encourage the children to color the masks. Help each child slip a drinking straw through the slits and tape it in place to make a handle for the mask. Be sure that each child's name is on the back of her or his mask.

Tell the children that Abraham was a man who did a lot of traveling in the desert. Invite the children to hold their camel masks in front of their faces (or let some children simply wave their masks if they are reluctant to put the masks over their faces).

Explain that you are all part of a camel caravan, a group of camels crossing the desert. You will start out, and everyone must follow you single file. Lead the class around your room. As you lead the group, describe the caravan in words such as the following. Add your own words and actions as needed.

> We are camels crossing the desert.
> Hear our feet on the sand? Scrunch, scrunch, scrunch!
>
> We can go a long ways without water,
> But sometimes we need a drink.
> Here's a palm tree by a well.
> Let's all take a drink. Slurp! Slurp! Slurp!
>
> Now it's time to cross some more desert.
> The sun is hot, and the sand blows
> Around our noses and our toes. Whoosh! Whoosh!
>
> We can close our noses to keep the sand out.
> We don't mind the sun and the sand.
> We just keep on walking. Scrunch, scrunch, scrunch!
> We are camels crossing the desert.

Bible
Genesis
18:1-15;
12:1-9;
21:1-7

© 2000 Abingdon Press.

14

Game 2

Walk Like a Camel

Show the children how to bend slightly at the waist and to do a bumpy/jerky kind of walk such as a camel would do in sand.

Let the children walk like camels as they follow you. Remind the children that camels are good animals to ride in the desert because they can go for a long time without water and they have big feet for walking in the sand.

Explain that you are all part of a camel caravan, a group of camels crossing the desert. You will start out, and everyone must follow you single file.

Lead the class around your room one or more times.

© 2000 Abingdon Press.

Game 3

The Laughing Game

Have the children join you on the rug or in an open area of the room. Choose one child to lie down on the floor, face up. Have the next child lie down with his or her head resting on the first child's stomach. The third person rests his or her head on the stomach of the second person, and so on.

As each child lies down, the person or persons on the floor should begin saying, "Ha, ha."

As each child joins the group, words of laughter will become true laughter as heads bounce on laughing stomachs. Join the game yourself after all of the other children are involved.

Say: God promised Sarah and Abraham that they would have children. They waited and waited and grew very old. Then God sent messengers to tell Abraham that Sarah would soon have a son. Sarah laughed when she heard the message because she was ninety years old, too old to have a baby. But God kept the promise, and Sarah had baby Isaac.

© 1999 Abingdon Press.

16

Permission granted to photocopy for local church use. © 2000 Abingdon Press.

Jacob's Dream

Game 1

Harump, Harump

Say: Jacob was a man who lived in Bible times. One day Jacob was going to another city. He traveled all day long. When people traveled in Bible times, sometimes they walked and sometimes they rode camels. Let's pretend that we are riding camels in a camel caravan.

Have the children pretend to ride camels and move about the room as you say the following movement poem.

Let's pretend we're riding camels,
Traveling over desert sands.
(*Pretend to ride camels; hold reins and gallop around the room.*)

Harump, harump.
Harump, harump.
(*Stop; sway back and forth.*)

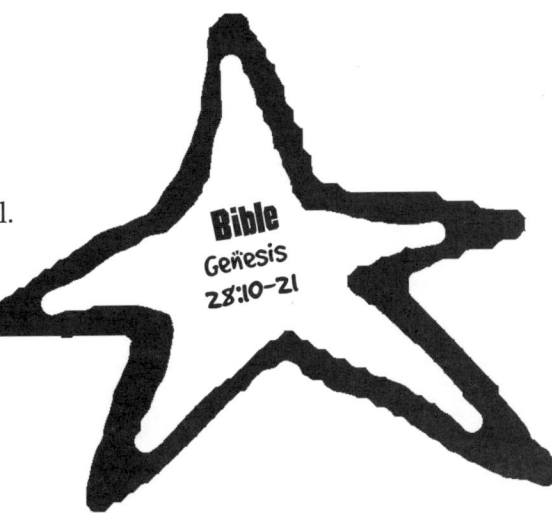

Say goodbye to friends and family
On our way to far-off lands.
(*Pretend to ride camels.*)

Harump, harump.
Harump, harump.
(*Stop; sway back and forth.*)

Sitting on the humps of camels,
Bouncing as they dip and sway.
(*Pretend to ride camels.*)

Harump, harump.
Harump, harump.
(*Stop; sway back and forth.*)

God is with us as we travel.
God is with us every day.
(*Pretend to ride camels.*)

Harump, harump.
Harump, harump.
(*Stop; sway back and forth.*)

© 1998 Abingdon Press.

Bible
Genesis
28:10-21

Game 2

Angel Antics

Enjoy using the following action verse with the children.

See the angels
(*Flap arms like wings.*)
Climb the ladder.
(*Pretend to climb up ladder.*)
Up and down,
(*Stretch up, squat down.*)
Up and down,
(*Stretch up, squat down.*)
Up and down they go.
(*Stretch up, squat down.*)

While Jacob's sleeping,
(*Put hand under head as if sleeping.*)
They climb the ladder.
(*Pretend to climb up ladder.*)
Up and down,
(*Stretch up, squat down.*)
Up and down,
(*Stretch up, squat down.*)
Up and down they go.
(*Stretch up, squat down.*)

© 1998 Abingdon Press.

Joseph and His Brothers

Game

Supplies: robe shakers (see page 20); crayons; scissors; construction paper in different colors; glue, tape, or stapler and staples

Joseph, Joseph

Photocopy and cut out the robe shakers (see page 20) for each child. Let the children decorate the robes with crayons. Show the children how to fold the robes along the dotted lines.

While the children are coloring, prepare one-inch strips of colored construction paper about six inches long. Help the children identify the colors, and let each child choose one color. Help the children glue, tape, or staple three or four of the same color strips to the bottom of their robes. Glue or staple the bottom of the robes together over the strips. Each child should have only one color of strips.

Show the children how to hold the robe part of their shakers. Practice shaking the colors with the children. Choose one child to be Joseph. Have the children hold their robe shakers and stand in a circle with Joseph in the middle.

Say the verse printed below.

> Joseph, Joseph, what's that color?
> What's that color on your coat?

Then shout out a color, such as: "It's red!" Have the children holding red robe shakers change places. Have Joseph try to get to one of the places in the circle before the switch is complete. The child left without a place becomes the next Joseph. Have the new Joseph stand in the middle of the circle and repeat the verse.

Continue the game, choosing different colors to switch places. Every once in a while, shout "All colors run!" and have everyone switch places.

Bible Genesis 37:12-28

© 1998 Abingdon Press

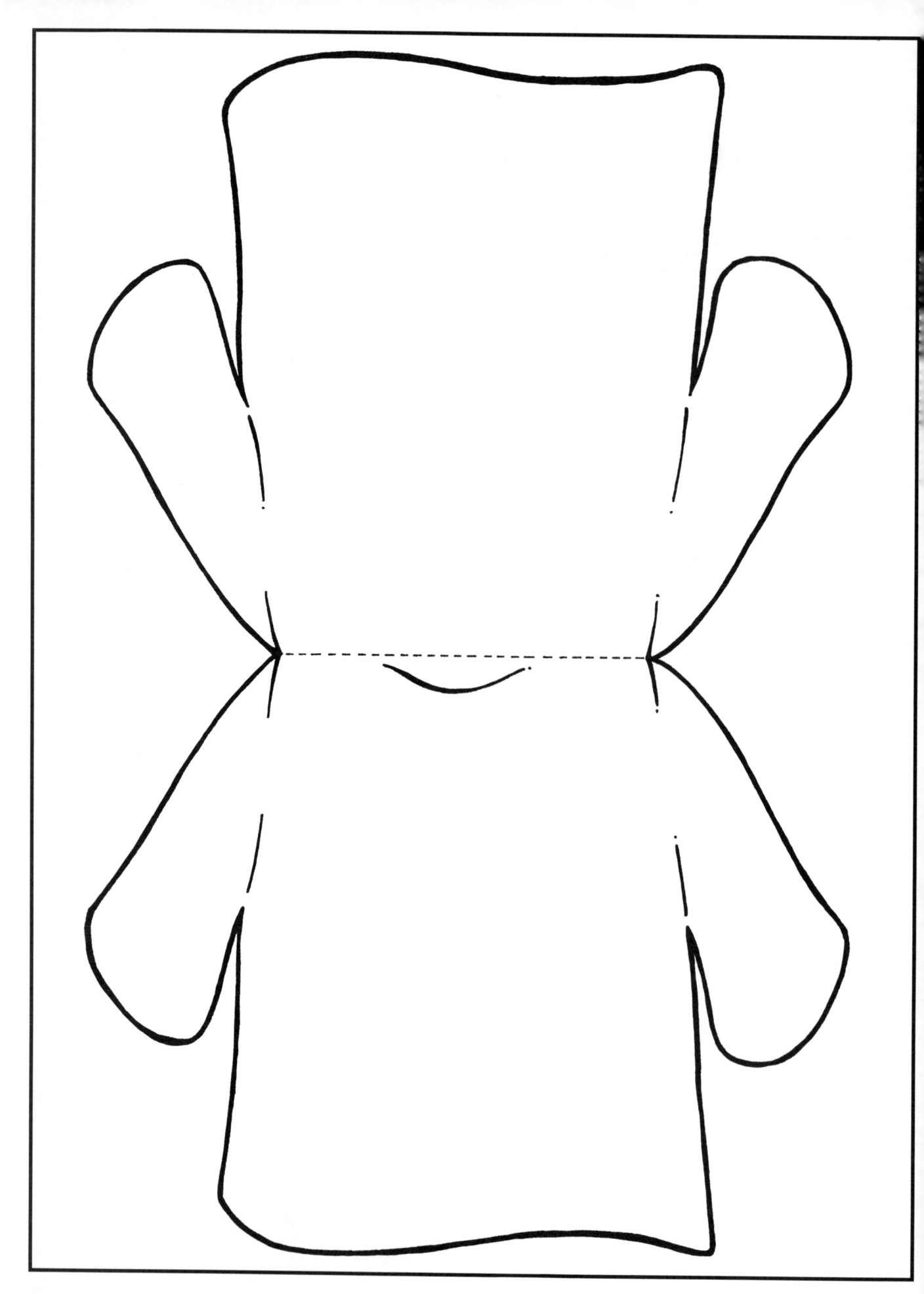

Permission granted to photocopy for local church use. © 1998 Abingdon Press.

Baby Moses

Game

Supplies: name cards (see page 22), scissors, marker, paper bag

Name Names

Photocopy and cut out the name cards (see page 22) so that you have one name card for each child. Use a marker to print each child's first name on a card. Mix the cards together and place them in a paper bag.

Have the children sit in a circle on the floor.

>**Say:** God planned for baby Moses to have a mother and sister, and for the princess to take care of him. God plans for us to have families to take care of us. God cares about families.

Pull a name card out of the bag. Help the children recognize the child's name printed on the card.

>**Say:** (*Child's name*) has a family. Who is in your family?

Let the child identify the persons in his or her family.

>**Say:** God cares about (*child's name*)'s family. (*Child's name*), stand up and hop around the circle.

Have the child named hop around the circle and then sit back down. Continue until every child has recognized his or her name card. Vary how you tell each child to move around the circle (gallop, tip-toe, march, jump, crawl, walk backwards, take giant steps, take baby steps, and so forth).

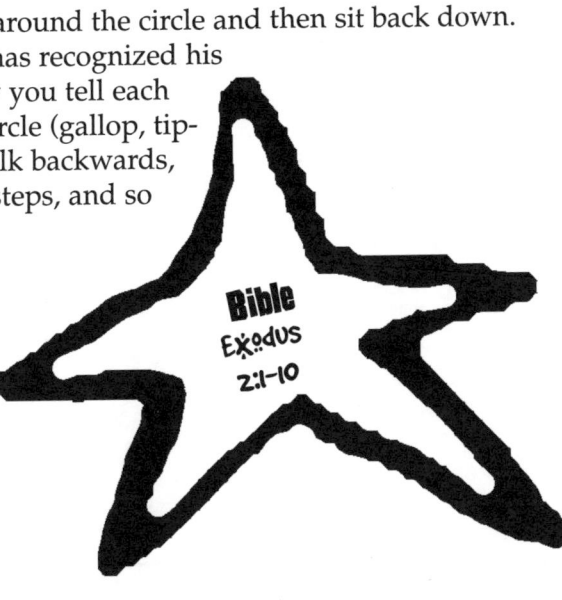

© 1998 Abingdon Press.

Bible
Exodus 2:1-10

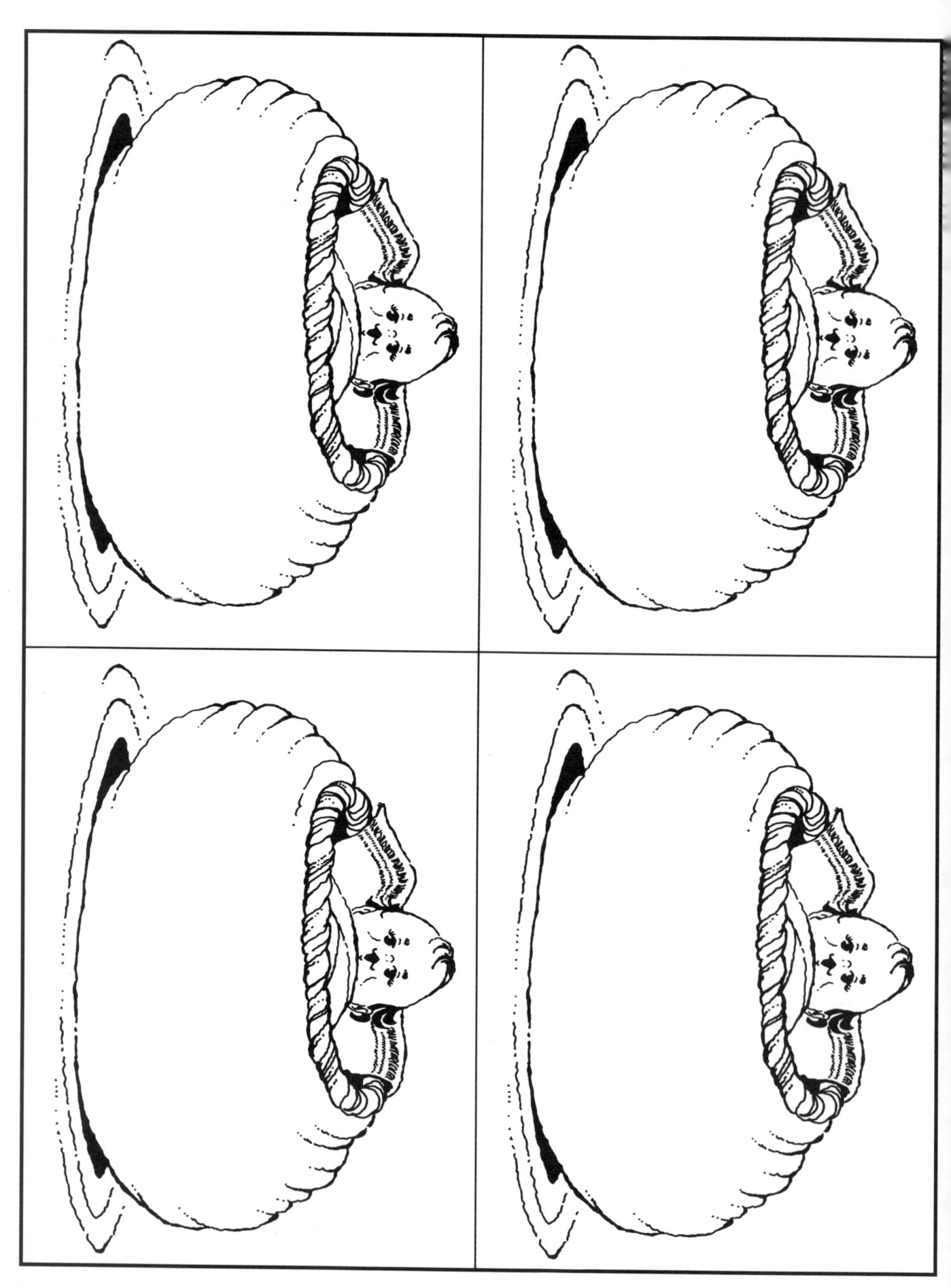

22 Permission granted to photocopy for local church use. © 1998 Abingdon Press.

The Burning Bush

Game

Supplies: bush picture (see page 24), scissors, glue, construction paper or posterboard, red tissue paper or construction paper, tape

Jump!

Before class begins, photocopy the bush picture (see page 24). Cut the picture into five pieces along the puzzle lines. Place the puzzle pieces picture-side down on the table.

Say: Let's try to guess what is pictured on this puzzle.

Choose a child to turn over one of the pieces. Have the children guess what the picture is. Continue to choose a child to turn over one piece of the puzzle and let the children guess what the picture is after the piece is turned over.

Help the children glue the puzzle pieces onto construction paper or posterboard. Show the children how to tear pieces of red tissue paper or construction paper into small pieces. Let the children glue the pieces onto the bush.

Have the children sit down in an open area. Tape the burning bush picture to the floor in front of the children.

Say: God wanted Moses to help the Hebrew people in Egypt. God wants us to help others. What are some ways we can help others?

Give the children an opportunity to respond.

Say: Listen carefully to what I say. If you think I am naming one way we can help others, stand up and jump over the burning bush. I will say your name when it is your turn.

Say: (Child's name), you help others when you pick up toys (set the table, pick up litter, put trash in the trash can, help your mom or dad cook, put your clothes away, help with the dishes, pray for family and friends).

Bible
Exodus 3:1-10

© 1998 Abingdon Press.

24 Permission granted to photocopy for local church use. © 1998 Abingdon Press.

Let My People Go!

Game 1

Supplies: fly and frog pictures (see page 26), scissors

Ribbit, Ribbit, Bzzz!

Before class begins, photocopy and cut apart the fly and frog pictures (see page 26). Have the children sit down in an open area of the room. Hold the fly and frog pictures in your hands like you were holding up a hand of cards. Choose a child to pick a card. Have the child show you the card, but not the other children. Encourage the child to pretend to be the animal pictured on the card. Let the other children guess whether the child is a fly or a frog.

Continue the game until each child has a turn.

Say: God used flies and frogs to help Moses make Pharaoh listen. We will find out about the flies and frogs in our Bible story.

© 1998 Abingdon Press.

Game 2

Croak 'n Creep

Have the children sit down on the floor. Choose one child to be Moses. Have Moses sit apart from the other children and close his or her eyes. Choose another child to be a frog.

Have the frog creep quietly around Moses and stop. Have the frog softly say, "Ribbit!" Have Moses point to where he or she thinks the frog is standing. Let Moses open her or his eyes.

Say: God was with Moses when he talked to Pharaoh. God is always with us. (*Child's name*) and (*child's name*), God is always with you.

Bible
Exodus 7:1-2;
8:1-6, 20-24

Continue the game until each child has a turn to be Moses or the frog.

© 1998 Abingdon Press.

25

26

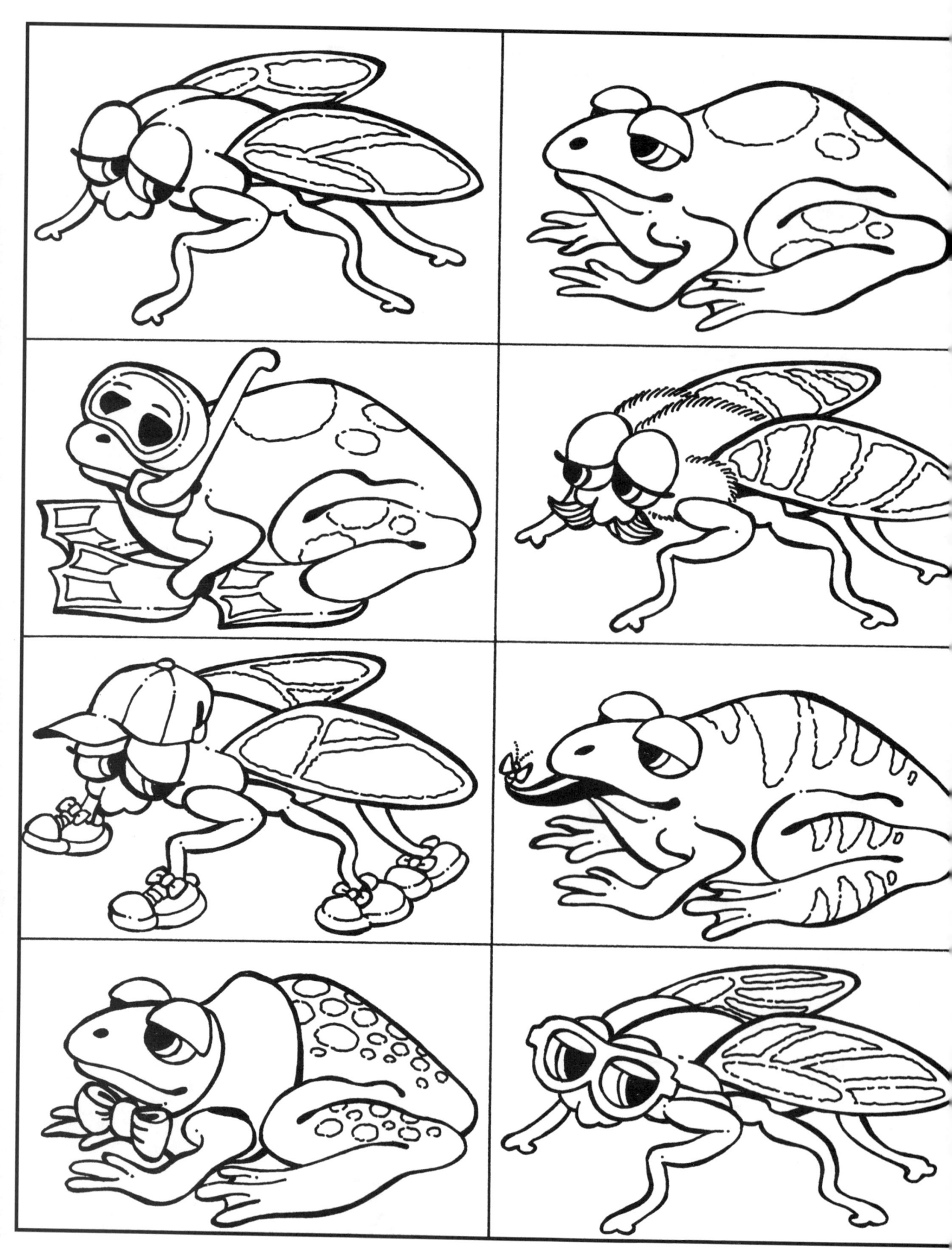

The Red Sea

Game 1

Red Sea Run

Have the children stand on one side of the room. You stand on the opposite side of the room. Choose a child to begin the game.

Say: (*Child's name*), (*child's name*), do you trust God? (*Have the child shout: "Yes!"*) Then run across the Red Sea.

Have the child run across the room to you. Play the game until each child has a turn. Vary the way you have the children cross the Red Sea (*tiptoe, march, hop, swim, walk backwards, take giant steps, take baby steps, crawl*).

© 1998 Abingdon Press.

Game 2

Supplies: large scarf or piece of rope

Jump Over the Sea

Have the children move to an open area of the room. Choose two children to be the Red Sea. Make sure there is space around the pair. Give the pair a scarf or rope about thirty-six inches long. Help the two children stand facing each other, each holding one end of the scarf or rope close to the floor. The children should stand far enough apart that the scarf or rope is pulled taut.

Say: God wanted Moses to lead the Hebrew people out of Egypt. Moses trusted God. He led the people out of Egypt across the Red Sea! Let's pretend to be Moses and the Hebrew people. Let's jump across the Red Sea. Each time someone jumps, let's shout, "Trust God!"

Have the children take turns jumping over the scarf or rope. After each child jumps, have all the children shout, "Trust God!" Choose two different children to hold the scarf or rope so that the first pair can have a turn jumping.

Bible
Exodus 14:1-22

© 1998 Abingdon Press.

# In the Wilderness

Game 1

Supplies: cassette or CD, cassette or CD player

Run, Quail, Run

Have the children move to an open area of the room.

Say: Let's pretend that you are quail and that I am Moses. Fly all around the room while I chase you. If I tag you, you must sit down on the floor.

Play music from a cassette or CD. Encourage the children to pretend to be birds flying around the room. Try to tag each child. When the child is tagged, have the child sit down where you tagged her or him. Play the game until every child is tagged.

Say: Today we're talking about a man named Moses. Moses led the Hebrew people out of Egypt into the wilderness. When the people were in the wilderness, they needed food to eat. God gave the people quail to eat.

© 1998 Abingdon Press.

Bible
Exodus
16:11-15

Game 2

Supplies: pictures of things we need (see page 30), scissors, tape

Picture Turnover

Photocopy and cut apart at least two sets of the pictures of things we need (see page 30). Tape one of the pictures to each child's clothing. There should be at least two children who have the same picture. Have the children stand in a circle.

> **Say:** God gave the Hebrew people food to eat in the wilderness. God gives us the things we need. We need sunshine, (*Have the children with the sun pictures raise their hands.*) animals, (*Have the children with the cat and dog pictures raise their hands.*) flowers, (*Have the children with the flower pictures raise their hands.*) food, (*Have the children with the food pictures raise their hands.*) water, (*Have the children with the glass of water pictures raise their hands.*) and people. (*Have the children with the people pictures raise their hands.*)

Sing the song below to the tune of "London Bridge" and have the children walk around the circle. Stop walking and name a picture on the last line. Have the children wearing that picture change places.

> God gives us the things we need,
> Things we need, things we need.
> God gives us the things we need,
> Things like (*name of picture*).

Repeat the song until you have named all the pictures.

Play the game again with additional movement. Call out the name of one of the pictures and tell the children how to move when they change places.

> **Say:** (*Name of picture*), hop! (*Suggest other motions like tiptoe, crawl, swim, walk backwards, fly, gallop, take giant steps, take baby steps, walk with your hands on your head, walk with hands on your hips, walk with hands on your knees, and so forth.*)

© 1998 Abingdon Press.

30
Permission granted to photocopy for local church use. © 1998 Abingdon Press.

The Ten Commandments

Game 1

Supplies: index cards, marker, masking tape

At—TEN—tion!

Write the numbers one through ten on separate index cards.

Place a line of masking tape on the floor. Make the line several feet long. Tape the number cards to the line in order from one to ten. Leave spaces between each card. Have the children line up at the beginning of the line.

Say: Today our Bible story is about the ten rules God gave Moses. Let's count to ten. (*Help the children count to ten.*)

Say each child's name and tell the child how to move down the line to a number.

(*Child's name*), jump to number four.
(*Child's name*), tiptoe to number seven.
(*Child's name*), crawl to number three.
(*Child's name*), pat your head and walk to number nine.
(*Child's name*), take baby steps to number two.
(*Child's name*), bend over and touch number one.
(*Child's name*), walk backwards to number five.
(*Child's name*), hop to number eight.
(*Child's name*), hold your ankles and walk to number six.
(*Child's name*), gallop to number ten.

© 1998 Abingdon Press.

Bible
Exodus 20:1-17

Game 2

Supplies: index cards, marker

Commandment Hop

Have the children move to an open area of the room. Write the numbers one through ten on separate index cards. Place the cards face down on the floor.

Say: God gave Moses ten rules to help the people live together.

Choose a child to begin. Have the child pick a number card. Show the children the number. Use the list of the Ten Commandments printed below. (The Commandments are paraphrased into simpler language for you to use with young children.)

Read the Commandment that corresponds with the number the child chose. Then have all the children hop the same number of times as the number of the Commandment. Continue until each child has had a turn to choose a card.

If you have a small group, let the children have more than one turn so that all ten cards are chosen at least once.

1. Love God.
2. Praise God.
3. Do not use God's name in a bad way.
4. Remember God on Sunday.
5. Love your mother and father.
6. Do not kill.
7. Love your wife or husband.
8. Do not take anything that doesn't belong to you.
9. Tell the truth.
10. Do not want what someone else has.

© 1998 Abingdon Press.

Joshua and the Walls of Jericho

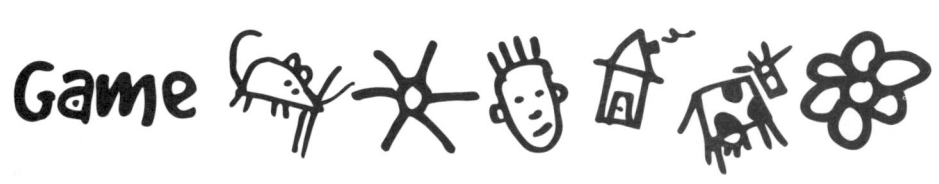

Game

Ring 'Round Jericho

Have the children stand in a circle and hold hands. Lead the children around the circle and recite the following rhyme:

> One time around the city walls,
> They marched round and round.
> One time around the city walls.
> Will the walls come falling down?

Have the children stop walking on the last line. Repeat the verse and have the children walk in a circle again. Change the number in the rhyme (two, three, four, five, six). On the seventh time use the stanza below and let the children fall down on the floor as in "Ring Around the Rosie."

> Seven times around the city walls,
> They marched round and round.
> Seven times around the city walls.
> See the walls come falling down!

If you prefer to play the game two times instead of seven times, begin with "Six times around the city walls."

Say: God told Joshua to march with the people around the walls of Jericho. Joshua trusted God and did what God wanted him to do.

© 1997 Abingdon Press.

Bible
Joshua
6:1-20

Serve the Lord

Game

Supplies: number cards (see page 35), scissors, masking tape

Number One

Photocopy and cut apart the number cards (see page 35). Make one set for each child in your class. Use masking tape to secure the numbers to the floor all around the room.

Help the children identify the numbers.

  Say: When you hear me call out a number, hop to that number.

Call out the number one. Have the children hop to the number one cards. Continue the game with numbers two, three, and four.

Then call out the number one again. Have the children hop to the number one cards. Have the children sit down on the number one cards.

  Say: We can tell others that there is only one God.

© 1999 Abingdon Press.

Bible
Joshua
24:15

Permission granted to photocopy for local church use. © 1999 Abingdon Press.

35

Ruth and Naomi

Game 1

Supplies: grain picture (see page 38), two baskets, scissors

Pass—It Basket

Photocopy and cut out the grain picture (see page 38) for each child. Put the pictures in a basket.

Have the children stand in a row. Give the first child in the row the basket with the grain pictures. Give the last child in the row an empty basket.

Say: Ruth was a woman who lived in Bible times. Ruth was kind to her mother-in-law, Naomi. She left her home and went with Naomi to a town called Bethlehem. When they got to Bethlehem, Ruth went to the fields to find grain so that she and Naomi could make bread to eat. Let's help Ruth pick the grain and take it home to Naomi.

Say the word *Go!* Have the first child pull a grain picture out of the basket and pass it along the row to the last child. Have the last child put the picture in the empty basket.

Continue until all the grain pictures have been passed down the row.

If time permits, have the child at the end of the row bring the basket with the grain pictures to the beginning of the row. Give the empty basket to the new child at the end of the row. Say, "Go!" and pass the grain pictures again.

© 1998 Abingdon Press.

Bible
Ruth
1–4

Game 2

Supplies: sequence cards (see page 39), scissors

Which Comes First?

Before class begins, photocopy the sequence cards showing steps in bread baking (see page 39) and cut them apart. Mix them up and place them face up on the table.

Talk about each of the pictures, asking the children what is pictured or what is happening in the picture. Point out that the oven is a Bible-times oven.

Help the children put the pictures in the correct sequence. When they have done so once, mix the pictures up and see if they can do so again. If you have a large class, make three or four sets of pictures and let the children work in small groups to put the pictures in sequence.

© 2000 Abingdon Press.

Game 3

Kindness Capers

Have the children sit in chairs in a circle.

Say: Let's think of some ways we can show kindness to others. If I say something that shows kindness, everyone stand up and clap your hands, then sit back down. If I say something that is not kind, everyone cross your arms and say, "No way!"

Say the statements below. Help the children know how to respond.

We can show kindness by helping Mom set the table for dinner.
We can show kindness by feeding our pets.
We can show kindness by not picking up our toys.
We can show kindness by helping Dad cook dinner.
We can show kindness by leaving our dirty clothes all over the floor.
We can show kindness by making a card to send to a friend.
We can show kindness by sharing toys with a friend.

© 1998 Abingdon Press.

38

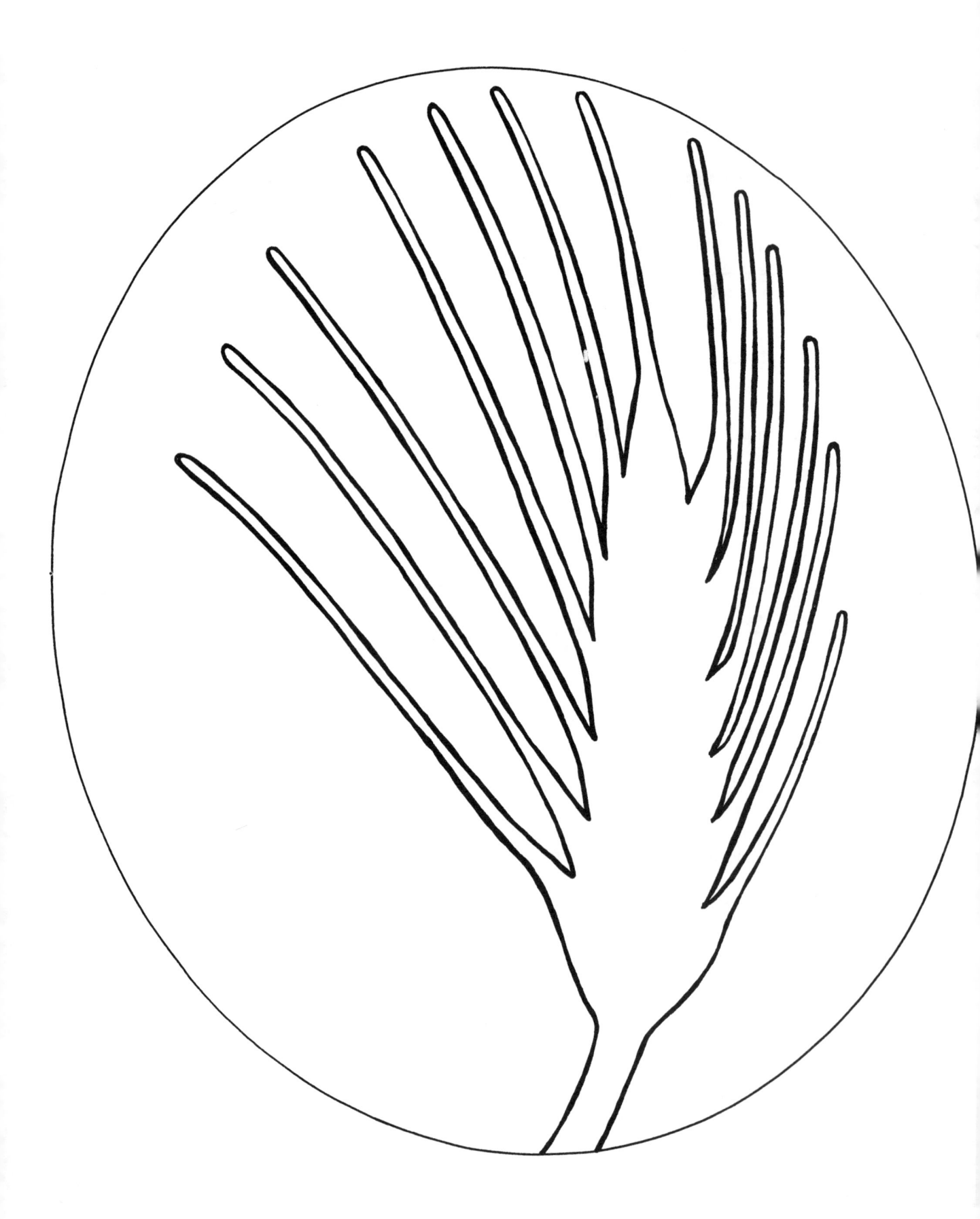

39

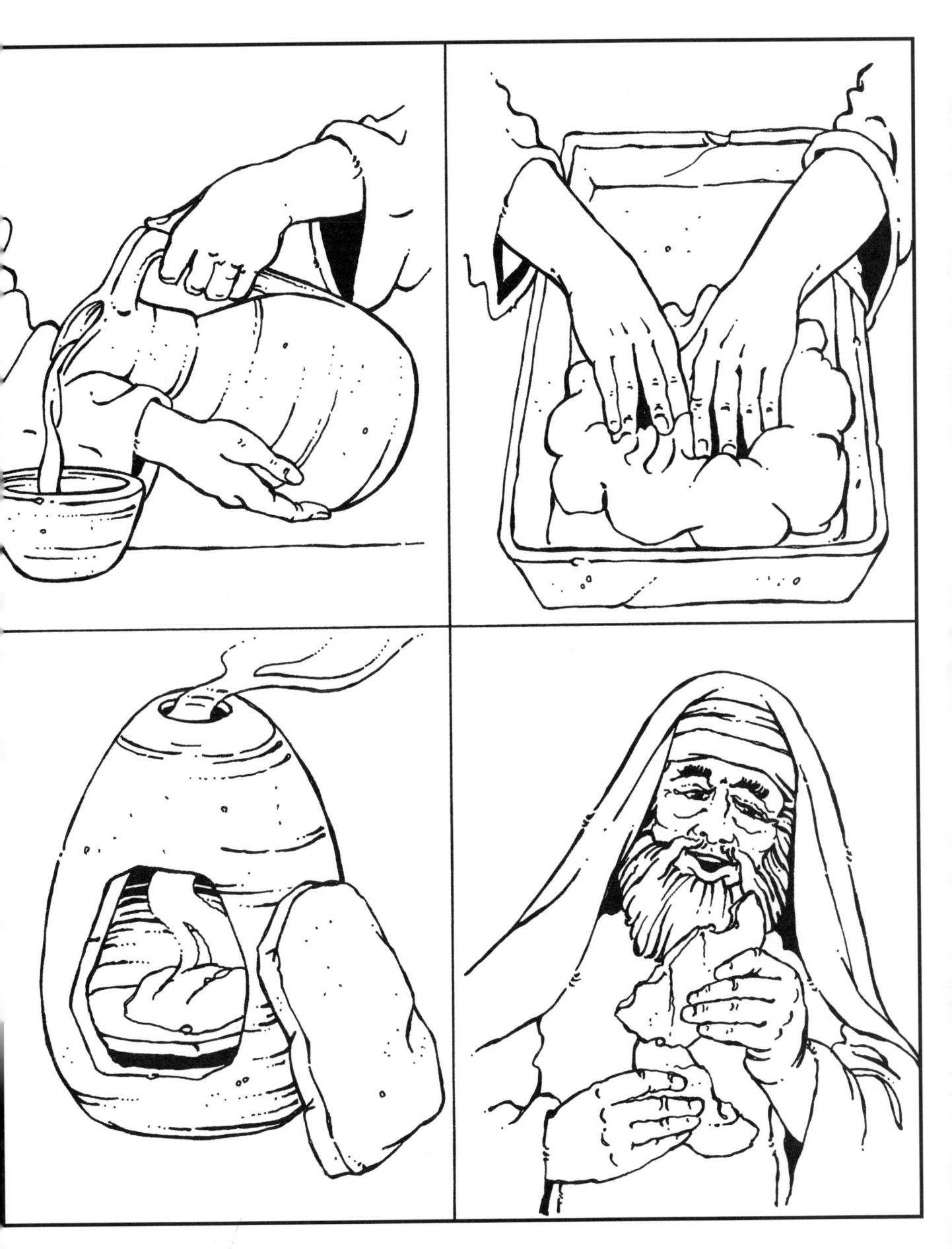

Hannah

Game 1

Supplies: masking tape, cassette or CD, cassette or CD player

Steppin' Out

Have the children move to one side of the room. Use masking tape to make a goal line on the other side of the room.

Say: Hannah wanted a baby. She prayed, and God answered her prayer. Hannah had a baby boy. She named her baby Samuel. Samuel grew, just like you grow. When you were a baby, you had to take baby steps. Now you can take giant steps.

Play music. Have the children take giant steps toward the line. Stop the music. When the music stops, have the children take baby steps toward the line. Alternate music and steps until all the children reach the line.

© 1998 Abingdon Press.

Game 2

Hannah's Hop

Say: Today we're hearing about a woman named Hannah. Hannah wanted a baby. She prayed to God, and God answered her prayer. Hannah had a baby boy. She named her baby Samuel. Samuel grew and grew.

Let the children hop around the room as you say the action poem below.

Hannah went to the temple
To talk to God in prayer.
So let's hop, hop here, (*Hop twice on one foot.*)
And hop, hop there, (*Hop twice on other foot.*)
And hop, hop everywhere. (*Hop twice on both feet.*)

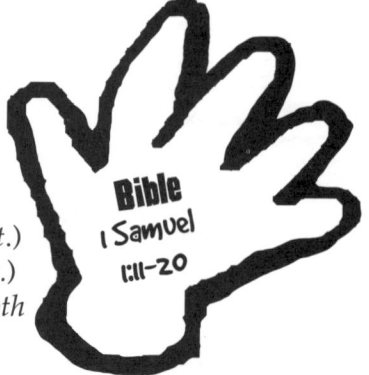

She asked God for a baby boy
'Cause she knew God answered prayer.
So let's hop, hop here, (*Hop twice on one foot.*)
And hop, hop there, (*Hop twice on other foot.*)
And hop, hop everywhere. (*Hop twice on both feet.*)

Bible
1 Samuel 1:11-20

Soon she had baby Samuel.
He was the answer to her prayer.
So let's hop, hop here, (*Hop twice on one foot.*)
And hop, hop there, (*Hop twice on other foot.*)
And hop, hop everywhere. (*Hop twice on both feet.*)

God was with Samuel as he grew.
Hannah thanked God with a prayer.
So let's hop, hop here, (*Hop twice on one foot.*)
And hop, hop there, (*Hop twice on other foot.*)
And hop, hop everywhere. (*Hop twice on both feet.*)

© 1998 Abingdon Press.

Game 3

Growing With God

Have the children move to an open area of the room.

Say: Today we're hearing about a woman named Hannah. Hannah wanted a baby. She prayed to God, and God answered her prayer. Hannah had a baby boy. She named her baby Samuel. Samuel grew and grew. God was with Samuel as he grew.

Say the following statements for the children and have the children do the motions. Give the children a few minutes to move around the room after each statement. Then have the children stop wherever they are in the room. Say, "God is with us as we grow!" and do the motion. Continue with the next statement and motion.

God is with us when we are babies. Let's crawl like babies.
(*Crawl around the room.*) Stop!
God is with us as we grow!
(*Crouch down and slowly stand with arms above head.*)

God is with us when we take our first steps. Let's walk with baby steps.
(*Take baby steps around the room.*) Stop!
God is with us as we grow!
(*Crouch down and slowly stand with arms above head.*)

God is with us when we grow big enough to march. Let's march.
(*March around the room.*) Stop!
God is with us as we grow!
(*Crouch down and slowly stand with arms above head.*)

God is with us when we grow big enough to gallop. Let's gallop.
(*Gallop around the room.*) Stop!
God is with us as we grow!
(*Crouch down and slowly stand with arms above head.*)

© 1998 Abingdon Press.

Samuel's Calling

Game

Listen 'n Do

Have the children move to an open area of the room.

Say: Today we're hearing about Samuel. Samuel grew from a baby to a boy. When Samuel was a boy, he helped Eli the priest in the temple. One night Samuel went to sleep on his mat. Then Samuel heard something that woke him up. Samuel had to listen very carefully to know what to do.

Say: Listen very carefully, and do what I tell you to do.

Call the children by name and give them two or three directions of things to do in sequence. Use the statements printed below as suggestions.

(*Child's name*), touch your nose, touch your elbow, and touch your knee.
(*Child's name*), hop on one foot, touch the floor, and turn around.
(*Child's name*), jump once, clap your hands, and touch the floor.
(*Child's name*), wiggle your hips, stomp your foot, and bend your knees.
(*Child's name*), touch your toes, touch your ear, and rub your stomach.
(*Child's name*), touch your head, jump once, and wiggle your hips.
(*Child's name*), touch the floor, touch your nose, and touch your ears.
(*Child's name*), stomp one foot, touch your knee, and jump three times.
(*Child's name*), wiggle your hips, turn around, and touch the floor.
(*Child's name*), hop on one foot, touch the floor, and turn around.

© 1998 Abingdon Press.

Bible
I Samuel
3:1-10

Samuel Finds David

Game 1

Supplies: heart crowns (see page 45); scissors; crayons; glue, tape, or stapler and staples; large basket or bag

Choosin' and Movin'

Photocopy and cut out the heart crown (see page 45) for each child. Give each child the heart piece. Let the children color the heart pieces with crayons.

Say: Today we're hearing about Samuel and David. Samuel grew into a man. When he was a man, God sent him to find a new king. God had Samuel choose a young boy named David to be the new king. God chose David because God knew David had a loving heart. That meant that David loved God and others.

Help each child glue, tape, or staple the ends of the crown pieces together to make one long strip. If you use staples, make sure the prongs of the staples are facing outward, away from the child's head. Write the child's name on the strip. Measure the crown strip around each child's head. Tape, glue, or staple the ends of the crown strip together. Have the children place their crowns in a large basket or bag.

Have the children move to one side of the room. Bring the heart crowns and move to the opposite side of the room. Pick up one of the crowns from the basket or bag. Notice the child's name.

Say: I am looking for someone with a happy smile and a loving heart. I choose (*child's name*). (*Child's name*), hop to me.

Have the child hop across the room to you. Place the crown on the child's head.

Say: (*Child's name*) has a loving heart. (*Child's name*) loves God and others.

Continue until every child has moved across the room and received his or her crown.

Vary how you tell each child to move (march, gallop, crawl, jump, walk on tiptoe, walk with giant steps, walk with baby steps).

Bible
1 Samuel 16:1-13

© 1998 Abingdon Press.

43

Game 2

David's Dance

Say: We're talking about Samuel and David. Samuel grew into a man. When he was a man, God sent him to find a new king. God had Samuel choose a young boy named David to be the new king. God chose David because God knew David had a loving heart. David loved God and others.

Lead the children in moving around the room as you say the following action poem for your children.

Step, step, step around the room. (*Walk around the room.*)
Now let's stop and sing. (*Stop, put hands around mouth.*)
David had a loving heart. (*Cross hands over heart.*)
God chose him to be king. (*Pretend to put crown on head.*)

March, march, march around the room. (*March around the room.*)
Now let's stop and sing. (*Stop, put hands around mouth.*)
David had a loving heart. (*Cross hands over heart.*)
God chose him to be king. (*Pretend to put crown on head.*)

Hop, hop, hop around the room. (*Hop around the room.*)
Now let's stop and sing. (*Stop, put hands around mouth.*)
David had a loving heart. (*Cross hands over heart.*)
God chose him to be king. (*Pretend to put crown on head.*)

© 1998 Abingdon Press.

Game 3

Hearts 'n Hands

Say: Having a loving heart means that we show love to God and to others. If I say something that shows love, clap your hands. If I say something that doesn't show love, keep your hands still.

We show love when we pray for one another. (*Clap hands.*)
We show love when we push and shove in line.
We show love when we share toys with our friends. (*Clap hands.*)
We show love when we sing praise to God. (*Clap hands.*)
We show love when we grab a toy away from a friend.
We show love when we say a Bible verse together. (*Clap hands.*)

© 1998 Abingdon Press.

Permission granted to photocopy for local church use. © 1998 Abingdon Press.

David and Jonathan

Game 1

Supplies: beanbags

Friendship Feats

Divide the children into pairs. Have each pair of friends stand on one side of the room. Make sure there is space to move between each pair.

Give each child a beanbag. Have each pair of children move together across the room as directed. Clap for all the children as they finish.

> Friends, hold the beanbag under your chins.
> Now walk across the room.
>
> Friends, hold the beanbag between your knees.
> Now hop across the room.
>
> Friends, hold the beanbag under your arms.
> Now tiptoe across the room.
>
> Friends, hold the beanbag with both hands.
> Now hop on one foot across the room.
>
> Friends, hold the beanbag behind your back.
> Now walk across the room.
>
> Friends, hold the beanbag behind your back.
> Now walk backwards across the room.
>
> Friends, hold the beanbag on top of your head.
> Now take baby steps across the room.
>
> Friends, hold your beanbag in one hand
>   and hold the hand of your friend with
>   the other hand.
> Now gallop together across the room.

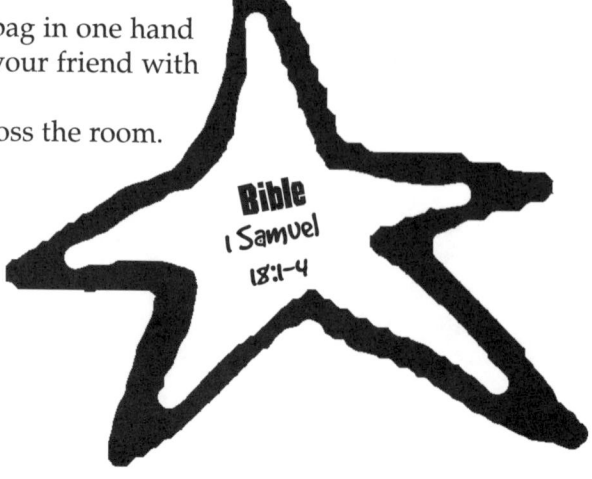

© 1998 Abingdon Press.

Bible
1 Samuel 18:1-4

Game 2

Friendship Follies

Divide the children into pairs and have them stand together in an open area of the room. Say the following statements and verse for the children. Have the children clap their hands and move as suggested.

A friend loves when you're sad.
A friend, a friend,
(*Clap hands on the word **friend**.*)
A friend loves at all times,
(*Clap hands on **friend** and **all**.*)
So let's get nose to nose.
(*Touch noses with partner.*)

A friend loves when you're happy.
A friend, a friend,
(*Clap hands on the word **friend**.*)
A friend loves at all times,
(*Clap hands on **friend** and **all**.*)
So let's get elbow to elbow.
(*Touch elbows with partners.*)

A friend loves when you're here.
A friend, a friend,
(*Clap hands on the word **friend**.*)
A friend loves at all times,
(*Clap hands on **friend** and **all**.*)
So let's get hip to hip.
(*Touch hips with partners.*)

A friend loves when you're away.
A friend, a friend,
(*Clap hands on the word **friend**.*)
A friend loves at all times,
(*Clap hands on **friend** and **all**.*)
So let's get knee to knee.
(*Touch knees with partners.*)

© 1998 Abingdon Press.

Solomon's Temple

Game 1

Temple Marching

Say: King Solomon had many workers build a special building called the Temple. It was a special place to worship and praise God. The workers cut boards from cedar trees, and they cut blocks of stone to make the Temple. Let's pretend we are workers marching to work on the Temple.

Have the children stand in a circle. Sing the following song to the tune of "Pop Goes the Weasel."

We're marching to Jerusalem. (*March around circle.*)
We're off to build the Temple. (*March around circle.*)
We'll build with boards (*Stop; pound one fist into other hand.*)
And big stone blocks. (*Lean over to touch floor as if picking up heavy stone.*)
Up goes the Temple! (*Pop straight up.*)

© 2000 Abingdon Press.

Game 2

King Solomon Says

Play "King Solomon Says" like "Simon Says." Have all the children stay in the game even if they make a mistake.

Say: King Solomon told his workers to build a beautiful Temple. Pretend I am King Solomon. When I say, "King Solomon says," do whatever I tell you to do. If I do not say, "King Solomon says," do not do what I tell you to do.

King Solomon says hop on one foot.
Clap your hands.
King Solomon says clap your hands.
King Solomon says touch the floor.
Stomp your feet.
King Solomon says stomp your feet.
King Solomon says turn around.
King Solomon says march.
King Solomon says sit down.

Bible
1 Kings
6:1-14;
8:62-63

© 2000 Abingdon Press.

Game 3

Supplies: crown (see page 50), scissors, paper-backed foil wrapping paper or colored construction paper, crayons or markers, glue sticks, large sequins, clear tape, masking tape

Royal Procession

Before class cut diamond shapes, circles, and ovals from paper-backed foil such as Christmas wrapping paper or from colored construction paper. Photocopy and cut out the crown and crown strip (see page 50) for each child.

Distribute the crown sections to the children. Put crayons or markers, glue sticks, the "jewels" you cut from paper, and large sequins in the center of the table.

Say: King Solomon was a king who lived long ago in Bible times. Kings wear crowns on their heads. Let's make King Solomon's crown.

Invite the children to color their crowns and to glue foil jewels and sequins on them with glue sticks. When each child is ready, use clear tape to put the two pieces of the child's crown together. Fit it to the child's head. Remove the crown and put a long strip of masking tape around the inside of the crown to strengthen it.

Have the children wear their crowns.

Say: King Solomon built a Temple where all the people could come and worship. Let's pretend we are people in Bible times. Let's go to the Temple to worship and praise God. Follow me and do what I do.

Lead the children around the room. Move your arm over your head, out to one side, behind your back, in front of one shoulder, and straight out in front of your body as you walk. Encourage the children to copy your motions.

© 2000 Abingdon Press.

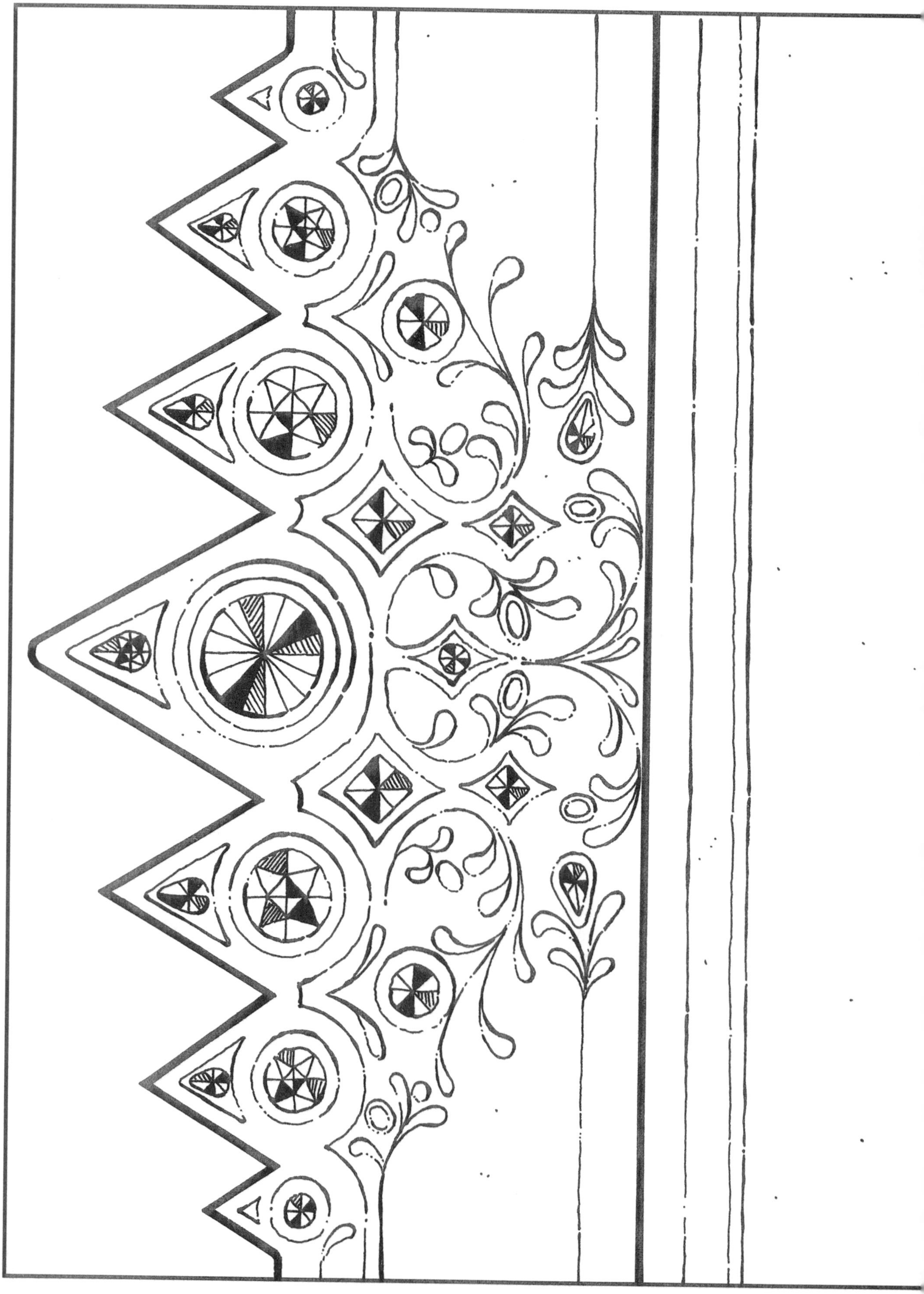

Esther

Game 1

Royal Romp

Say: Let's have a royal parade. Let's all follow Queen Esther.

Let a child be Queen Esther. Hold the child's hand and lead the children in following the leader. Wind the children around the room, circling chairs and tables. Change how you move (walk, hop, tiptoe, march) and have the children copy the movements. Sing "Follow Me" to the tune of "London Bridge."

> Follow me, for I am queen,
> I am queen, I am queen.
> Follow me, for I am queen.
> I help my people. (*Stand still and wave like a beauty queen.*)

After each time you stop and wave, choose a different child to be Queen Esther. If you have a large number of children, play the game and be Queen Esther yourself.

© 1997 Abingdon Press.

Game 2

Queen Esther, Queen Esther

Choose one child to be Queen Esther. Have Queen Esther stand in front of the group. Repeat the rhyme below.

> Queen Esther, Queen Esther, you are so brave.
> What did you do, your people to save?

Have the child choose a movement he or she wants to do, such as jumping, hopping, clapping, or turning around. If needed, give suggestions. Have the child pretending to be Queen Esther begin. Have the other children follow. Choose another child to be Queen Esther. Play as long as the children show interest.

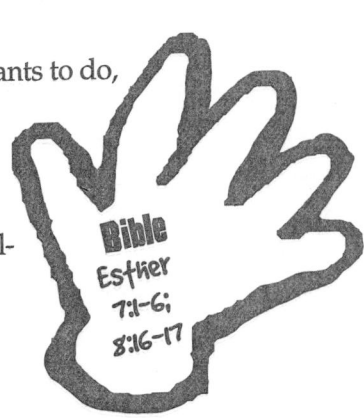

© 1997 Abingdon Press.

Bible Esther 7:1-6; 8:16-17

Jeremiah

Game 1

Jeremiah Jump

Have the children move to an open area of the room and sit down.

Say: God wanted Jeremiah to tell people about God, but Jeremiah thought he was too young. God told Jeremiah he was old enough. We are big enough to tell others about God. I will name a color and ask, "Can you tell others about God?" If you are wearing the color, jump up and shout, "Yes, we can!"

Continue, naming different colors until all the children have had a turn.

© 1999 Abingdon Press.

Game 2

Supplies: beachball

Big Ball Bop

Say: When you were babies, you were too small to do many things. You were too small to walk by yourself; you were too small to jump and run. But now you are big enough to do all those things.

Choose a child to begin the game.

Say: (*Child's name*), let's see if you are big enough to roll this ball across the room.

Give the child the beachball. Have the child roll the ball across the room.

Say: Yes! (*Child's name*) is big enough to roll the ball.

Continue the game until each child has had a turn with the ball.

Say: Today we're hearing about a young man named Jeremiah. God told Jeremiah that he was old enough to tell others about God.

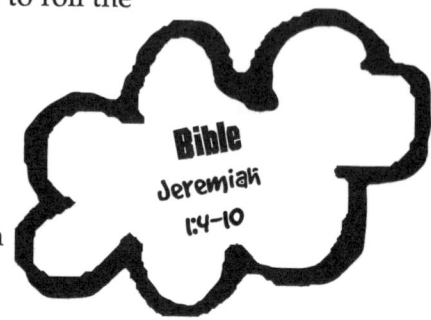

Bible
Jeremiah 1:4-10

Potters

Game 1

Supplies: pottery cards (see page 54), scissors, basket

Pottery Match

Before class make four or five photocopies of the pottery cards (see page 54) and cut the cards apart. Place the cards face up on the table.

Say: Here are pictures of things that a potter in Bible times could make on his potter's wheel. There are jugs and jars and bowls. Can you match them?

Invite the children to sort the cards and to make piles of matching pottery vessels. Encourage them to count the number of vessels in each pile.

Put two matching cards for every two children in a basket. (Include yourself if you have an uneven number of children.) Mix up the cards and let each child draw one. Have each child try to find the person who has a matching card. If you have a large class, use three or four cards for every three or four children. In that case it won't matter if one group has fewer children.

© 2000 Abingdon Press.

Game 2

Supplies: pottery cards (see page 54); scissors; plastic play coins, checkers, or small juice can lids

To Market, To Market

Use the same pottery cards as in the previous activity. Let the children sort them into piles again.

Say: When the potter made lots of bowls and jugs, he sold them at the village market. Sometimes he put a rug on the ground and piled his jugs on it for people to look at and to buy from him.

Let the children take turns being the pottery seller and selling cards to the other children. Hand out plastic play coins, checkers, or small juice can lids for the children to use as money.

Bible
Jeremiah 18:1-6

© 2000 Abingdon Press.

Permission granted to photocopy for local church use. © 2000 Abingdon Press.

Jonah

Game 1

Jonah-in-the-Fish

Say: Jonah was swallowed by a great big fish. Let's pretend to be Jonah sitting in the fish.

Have the children fold their hands as if praying and crouch down while you say the first three lines of the rhyme. On the last line have the children jump up and say, "Yes, I will!"

Jonah-in-the-fish,
Sitting so still,
Won't you go to Ninevah?
Yes, I will!

© 1997 Abingdon Press.

Game 2

Obey Simon

Have the children move to an open area of the room. Play "Simon Says" with the children.

Say: Let's play "Simon Says." In this game you must obey Simon and do what Simon tells you to do. Only move when I say, "Simon says." If I do not say, "Simon says," don't do the motion.

Use the suggestions on the following page to play the game with the children. Do not make the game a competition. Let everyone stay in the whole game. When the children make a mistake, say something like, "Some of us didn't obey Simon. Let's try again."

Bible
Jonah
1:1—3:3

Simon says put your hands on your head.
Simon says touch your toes.
Touch your knees. (*Don't move.*)
Simon says shake your hands.
Simon says hop up and down.
Simon says touch your nose.
Touch your elbow. (*Don't move.*)
Touch your ears. (*Don't move.*)
Simon says wiggle your whole body.
Simon says sit down.

© 1999 Abingdon Press.

Game 3

Yes!

Have the children stand in an open area of the room.

Say: Our Bible tells us to obey God and our parents. Let's practice obeying God and our parents.

Say the response verse printed below. Have the children respond as suggested.

Dad tells you to go to bed.
To obey, what do you say?
Yes, Dad! (*Shake hands at knee height.*)

Mom asks you to stay in the back yard.
To obey, what do you say?
Yes, Mom! (*Shake hands at shoulder height.*)

God wants you to learn from the Bible.
To obey, what do you say?
Yes, God! (*Shake hands above head.*)

Yes, Dad! (*Shake hands at knee height.*)
Yes, Mom! (*Shake hands at shoulder height.*)
Yes, God! (*Shake hands above head.*)

© 1999 Abingdon Press.

NEW TESTAMENT

The Wise Men

Game 1

Gift Exchange

Say: The wise men gave Jesus three gifts. The gifts were gold, frankincense, and myrrh.

Have the children repeat the names of the gifts.

Say: Let's pretend to be the three gifts.

Have the children stand in a circle. Go around the circle and say the name of one of the gifts for each child. Have that child repeat the name. Explain that each child needs to remember the name of his or her gift.

Say: Gold and frankincense, change places.

All the children who are named gold and frankincense should change places.

Continue the game, calling out the names of the gifts and having the children change places. Sometimes call only one name; sometimes call all three.

© 1999 Abingdon Press.

Bible
Matthew
2:1-11

Game 2

Supplies: stars (see page 60), scissors, yarn or tape, crayons

Star Stretch

Photocopy the stars (see page 60). Cut out the stars. Cut yarn into lengths to hang the stars just out of reach of your children.

You might hang the stars from your ceiling or from a clothesline stretched across your room. Hang the biggest star higher than the other stars.

As the children enter the room, encourage the children to jump up to touch the stars. Have the children jump up higher to try to touch the biggest star.

Or photocopy the stars and do not cut them out. Tape the star pages to the underside of a classroom table. Cover the underside completely with star pages. Let the children take turns lying on their backs underneath the table and using crayons to color the stars.

Say: The wise men followed a star to find Jesus. When they found Jesus in a house in Bethlehem, they worshiped Jesus and gave him gifts.

© 1997 Abingdon Press.

Permission granted to photocopy for local church use. © 1997 Abingdon Press.

The Beatitudes

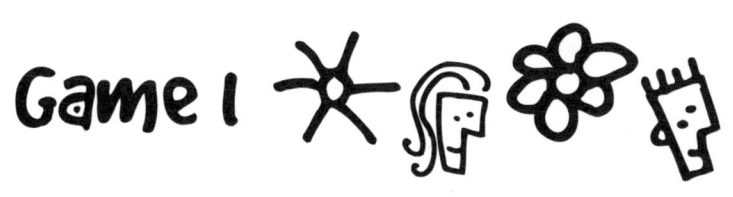

Game 1

Supplies: happy face and heart (see page 63), scissors, crayons or markers, tape

Happy Faces, Happy Hearts

Photocopy and cut out the happy face and the heart (see page 63) for each child. Give each child the happy face. Let the children decorate the happy face with crayons or markers.

Say: When Jesus taught in the synagogue, he told the people good news.

Tape the happy face to the back of each child. Tape a heart to the front of each child.

Say: The good news Jesus told the people was that God loves each one of us.

Have the children line up in an open area of the room. Explain to the children that when they hear you say the words *happy faces*, they are to turn around to show the happy faces taped on their backs. When they hear you say the words *happy hearts*, they are to turn to show the hearts taped to their fronts. Have the children repeat the last two lines.

Say the poem below for the children. Have them move as suggested. Repeat the poem several times.

Happy faces, happy hearts,
(*Turn to back; turn to front.*)
Can you tell the two apart?
The happy face says we have good news.
(*Turn to the back to show happy faces.*)
The happy heart says God loves you!
(*Turn to the front to show hearts.*)

Good news! God loves you!
(*Have the children repeat the phrase.*)
Good news! God loves you!
(*Have the children repeat the phrase.*)

Bible
Matthew
5:3-12

© 1997 Abingdon Press.

Game 2

Happy Hands

Have the children sit down on the floor.

Say: Listen carefully as I sing a song. If you are wearing something that is the color I name, stand up. When I ask you to "tell me that you're happy," the children that are standing up can say, "I am very happy."

Sing the following song to the tune of "Are You Sleeping?"

Who's wearing yellow?
Who's wearing yellow?
Please stand up. (*Children wearing yellow stand up.*)
Please stand up.
Tell me that you're happy.
(*Children wearing that color*): **I am very happy**.
Sit back down.
Sit back down.

Sing the song and name different colors until everyone has had at least one turn to stand up.

© 1998 Abingdon Press.

Game 3

Supplies: triangle (see page 64), scissors, crayons, tape

Happy Hero Hop

Photocopy and cut out the triangle (see page 64) for each child. Let the children color the triangle with crayons. Tape the triangle onto the front of each child's clothing. Have the children sit down in an open area of the room.

Say: One of the things Jesus taught his friends was that people who do what God wants them to do are happy. If I say something that you think God wants us to do, jump up and say, "Be happy and glad!"

Share your toys. (*Jump.*)
Be happy and glad!
Be kind. (*Jump.*)
Be happy and glad!
Take turns. (*Jump.*)
Be happy and glad!

© 1998 Abingdon Press.

63

64

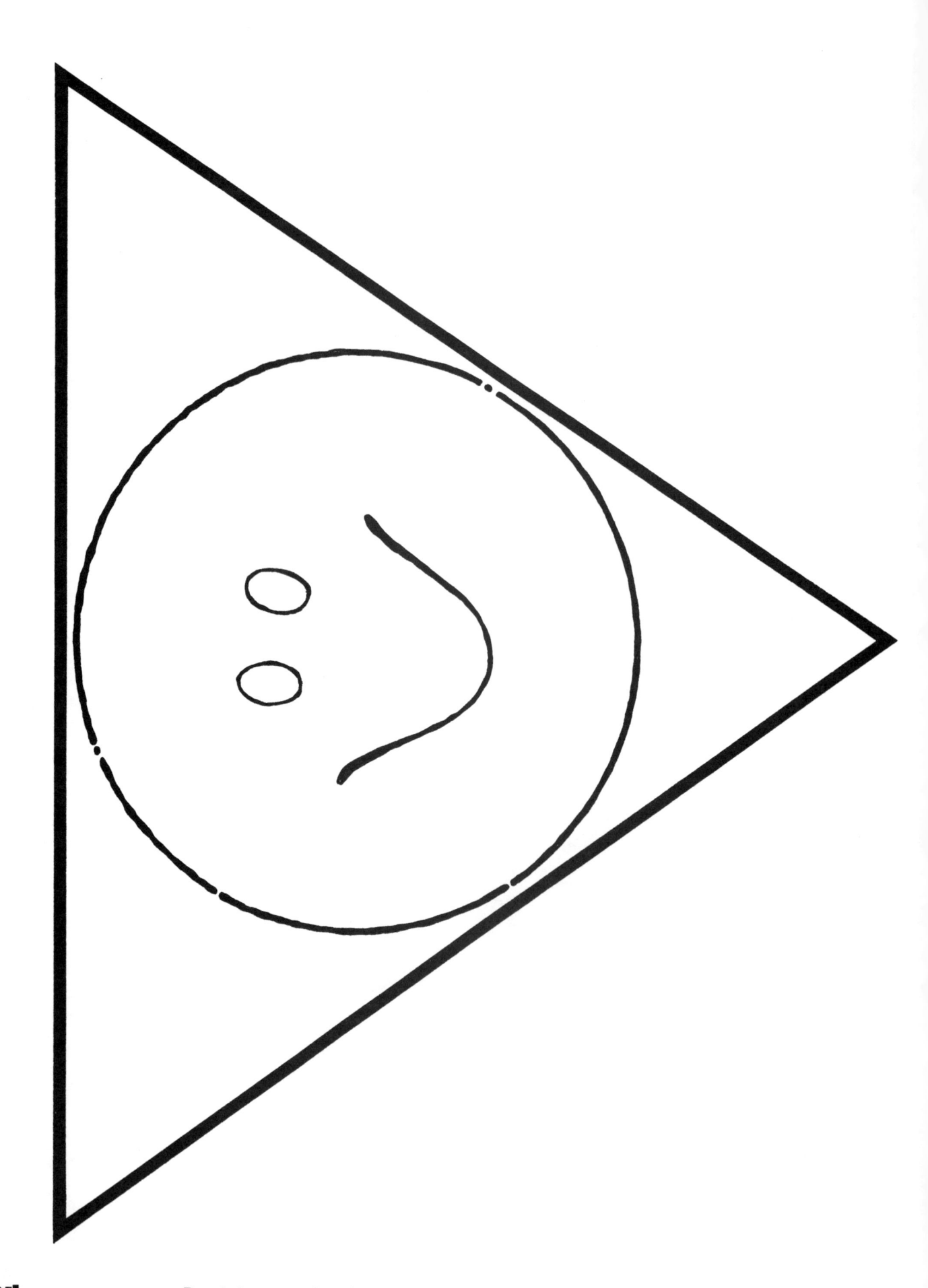

The Least of These

Game

Birds Fly Like This

Have the children move to an open area of the room.

Say: Jesus said that God cares about the birds and flowers. Let's pretend that we are birds.

Birds fly like this. (*Have the children flap their arms like bird wings.*)

Birds fly and hop like this. (*Have the children flap their arms and hop up and down at the same time.*)

Birds fly and hop and wiggle their tail feathers like this. (*Have the children flap their arms, hop up and down, and wiggle their backsides at the same time.*)

Birds fly and hop and wiggle their tail feathers and eat like this. (*Have the children flap their arms, hop up and down, wiggle their backsides, and nod their heads up and down as if pecking food at the same time.*)

Birds fly and hop and wiggle their tail feathers and eat and then go to sleep like this. (*Have the children flap their arms, hop up and down, wiggle their backsides, and nod their heads up and down as if pecking food at the same time. Then have the children sit down, tuck their heads under their arms, and pretend to sleep.*)

Say: Then Jesus said that God cares even more about people. We know God cares for each one of us.

© 1998 Abingdon Press.

Bible
Matthew 6:25-31

The Lost Sheep

Game 1

Supplies: stuffed lamb (or other stuffed animal)

Sheep Search

Have the children sit down. Show the children the stuffed lamb (or other stuffed animal). Choose one child to be the shepherd. Have the shepherd go with a teacher out of the room or hide his or her eyes with both hands. Hide the lamb somewhere in the room.

Have the shepherd come back into the room or uncover her or his eyes. Have the shepherd look for the lamb. When the shepherd is close to the lamb, have the other children *baa* like sheep. When the shepherd moves away from the lamb, have the children stay quiet. Have all the children clap their hands when the shepherd finds the lamb.

Say: God is like a shepherd who takes care of the sheep.

Repeat the activity until everyone has had a chance to find the sheep. (Hint: If you have a team teacher or helper, that person can take the finder outside the room while you and the remaining children hide the lamb.)

© 2000 Abingdon Press.

Bible
Matthew 18:10-14

Game 2

Yes!

Have the children sit down.

Say: Shepherds and sheep were important in Bible times. Jesus told the story about a lost sheep to show what God is like. Jesus said that God cares for everyone just as the shepherd cared for the sheep. I am going to ask you some questions. I want you to answer each question by jumping up and shouting, "Yes!" Then sit down again.

Does God care for old people?
Does God care for babies?
Does God care for people who use wheelchairs?
Does God care for people with no hair?
Does God care for you?

© 2000 Abingdon Press.

Game 3

Fuzzy Wuzzy Was a . . .

Say: Jesus told a story about a shepherd and a lost sheep. The shepherd took care of the sheep and loved the sheep. God is like the shepherd.

Encourage the children to move around the room and to pretend to be sheep. Allow the children time to pretend.

Say: Come, little sheep, follow me. I am your shepherd. (*Lead the children around the room. Stop in one corner of the room.*) Come and eat, little sheep, eat the sweet-tasting grass. (*Lead the children to another area of the room.*) Come and drink, little sheep, drink the cool water from the stream. (*Lead the children to a rug.*) Now rest, little sheep, lie down and sleep in the warm sun.

© 1998 Abingdon Press.

Forgive One Another

Game 1

Cat and Mouse

Have the children sit in a circle on the floor.

Say: Let's pretend to be cats and mice. The cats will ask the mice to forgive.

Select one child to be the cat and to move to the center of the circle. All the children sitting in the circle will be the mice. Have the cat kneel in front of one of the mice in the circle (in any order at all).

Have the cat say: "Meow, meow! Please forgive me!" Have the mouse pat the cat on the head, and say, "Squeak, squeak! I forgive you." Then have the cat chase the mouse around the circle.

If the cat tags the mouse before he or she can sit back down in the circle, the mouse becomes the new cat.

Continue until everyone has had an opportunity to be the cat.

© 1999 Abingdon Press.

Game 2

Feelings Follies

Have the children stand in a circle.

Say: Jesus taught us to forgive one another. How do you think it feels to forgive someone? (*Let the children respond.*) I think forgiving someone feels like a smile. Let's send smiles around our circle.

Turn to one of the children next to you. Smile at the child. Have that child turn to the next child and smile. Continue around the circle. Continue the game with other statements and motions.

Say: I think forgiving someone feels like: a handshake, (*Shake hands around the circle.*) a pat on the back, (*Pat around the circle.*); and a hug. (*Hug around the circle.*)

© 1998 Abingdon Press.

Bible Matthew 18:21-22

Game 3

Supplies: index cards, brown paper bag, marker (optional: cassette or CD, cassette or CD player)

Smile! Jesus Loves . . .

Write each child's name in large block letters on an index card. Place all the cards inside a brown paper bag. Have the children sit in a circle on the floor. Show the children the bag.

Say: Today we learned that Jesus wants us to forgive. Jesus was a special teacher. He taught us about God and God's love. We know that Jesus loves each one of us.

Pass the bag around the circle. Play music from a cassette or CD, or sing "Jesus Loves Me." Stop the music. Have the child holding the bag reach in and pull out a name card. Say the name printed on the card. Have that child stand up.

Say: (*Child's name*), Jesus loves you. Thank you, God, for Jesus and for (*child's name*). Amen.

Repeat the game until every name has been drawn from the bag and you have prayed for every child.

© 1998 Abingdon Press.

The Withered Hand

Game 1

Supplies: objects such as crayons, paper clips, or scraps of paper; box lid or basket; large pair of gloves

Glove Grab

Place several objects on the table or rug. You might use crayons, paper clips, or scraps of paper. Have a box lid or basket on the table or rug. Have each child place his or her hands inside a large pair of gloves.

Let each child use his or her gloved hands to try to pick up the objects and place them in the basket. Then have the child take off the gloves and pick up the objects with her or his bare hands. Talk with the children about how much easier it was to pick things up with their bare hands.

Say: Today we're talking about Jesus and a man who could not move his hand. Jesus touched the man's hand and healed the hand so that it could move again. Jesus helped the man.

© 1998 Abingdon Press.

Game 2

Supplies: construction paper, crayons or markers, tape

Handy Work

Give each child a piece of construction paper. Have the child place a hand on the paper with her or his fingers spread out.

Trace around the child's hand with

Bible
Mark 3:1-5

a crayon. Write the child's name underneath the handprint. Let the children decorate their handprints with crayons or markers. Place loops of tape on the back of the handprint.

Help each child tape his or her handprint on the floor. Make sure there is moving space around each handprint.

Say: Today we're hearing about Jesus and a man who could not move his hand. Jesus touched the man's hand and healed the hand so that it could move again. Jesus helped the man.

Have the children stand next to their handprints.

Say: Do what I tell you to do. When I say, "Touch your hand," put your hand on your handprint. (*Demonstrate putting your hand on a handprint.*)

Give the children the directions printed below. Start out speaking slowly and then talk faster as the children learn the game.

Say: Touch your knees. Touch your head. Touch your nose. Touch your hand. Touch your hips. Touch your toes. Touch your backside. Touch your hand. Touch your shoulders. Touch your ear. Touch your hand.

© 1998 Abingdon Press.

Game 3

Supplies: animal pictures and hand signs (see pages 72 and 73), scissors

Handtalk Zoo

Photocopy and cut apart the animal pictures and hand signs (see pages 72 and 73). Have the children sit in a circle.

Choose one child to begin. Have the child come to you and pick an animal card. Help the child identify the animal without showing the card to the rest of the children. Let the child move into the center of the circle and act out the animal. Have the other children guess the animal. Have the child sit back down.

Teach the children the hand sign for the animal. Continue until each child has had a turn.

Say: Our hands are very important. We use our hands to touch and to pick up things. Sometimes people talk with their hands. Talking with your hands is called sign language. We just learned how to say some animal names in sign language. Today we're talking about Jesus and a man who could not move one of his hands. Jesus helped the man.

71

bug	kangaroo
tiger	elephant
butterfly	monkey

72
Permission granted to photocopy for local church use. © 1998 Abingdon Press.

bear	spider
bird	rooster
owl	cat

Two by Two

Game 1

Traveling Twofers

Tell the children that Jesus sent his followers out two by two. Ask them to pretend to be your followers and to join hands and do as you say when you call their names.

Give instructions such as the following:

(*Child's name*) and (*child's name*), skip to the door and back.
(*Child's name*) and (*child's name*), find something red and bring it to me.
(*Child's name*) and (*child's name*), hop around the table one time.
(*Child's name*) and (*child's name*), sit down on the same chair.
(*Child's name*) and (*child's name*), make funny faces to make each other laugh.
(*Child's name*) and (*child's name*), march across the room and back.

© 2000 Abingdon Press.

Bible
Mark
6:7-13

Game 2

Supplies: traffic lights (see page 76), green and red markers, tape or stapler and staples

Traffic Light Tiptoe

Photocopy the traffic lights (see page 76). Color the bottom light of one traffic light green. Color the top of the second traffic light red.

Fold the traffic lights along the center line. Tape or staple the sides of the traffic lights together. Put your hand in the bottom opening of the traffic light.

Say: Jesus told his helpers to go to all people everywhere and tell them about Jesus.

Ask: What are some things we can tell our friends and families about Jesus? (*Help the children think of things to say about Jesus, such as, "Jesus loves me"; "Jesus is God's son"; "Jesus loves children"; and so forth.*)

Have the children move to one side of the room.

Say: Let's play a game. When I hold up the green light, (*Show the children the green light side of the traffic light.*) everyone may tiptoe across the room to me. When I hold up the red light, (*Show the children the red light side of the traffic light.*) everyone must stop. Before we can go again, I want each of you to tell me one thing about Jesus.

Hold up the green light. Have the children tiptoe across the room. Turn the traffic light to the red light. Have the children stop. Name each child and ask him or her to tell you one thing about Jesus.

Turn the traffic light to the green light.

Say: Now hop across the room.

Continue playing the game as the children show interest. Vary how the children are to move across the room (crawl, take giant steps, take baby steps, gallop, walk backwards, walk with hands on head).

© 1999 Abingdon Press.

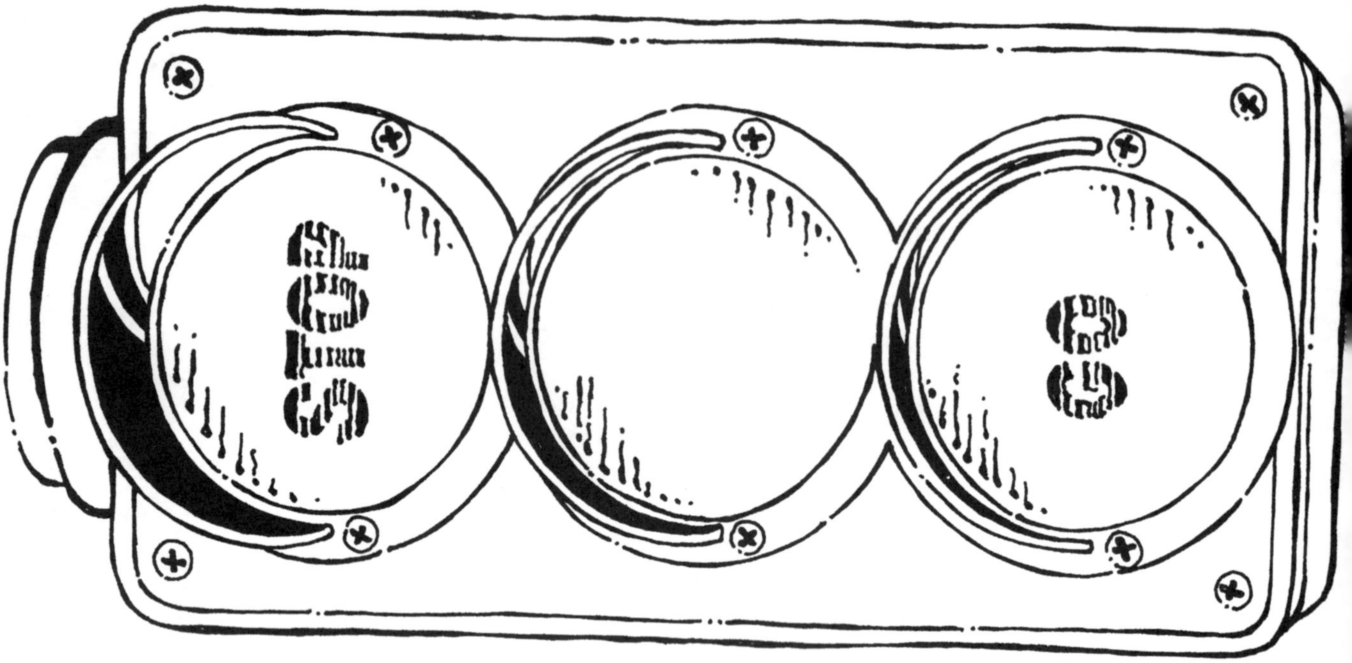

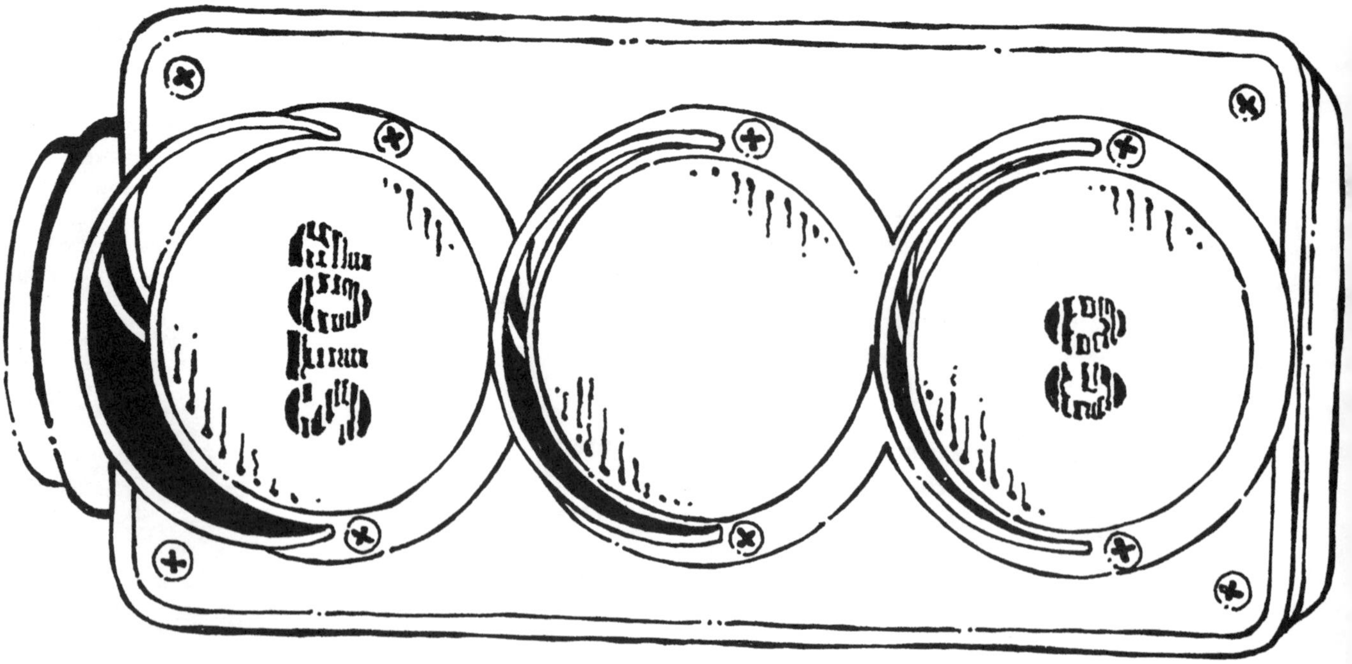

Jesus and the Children

Game 1

Through the Crowd

Choose one child to be the leader. Have the other children line up behind the leader. Instruct the children to stand with their feet apart to make a tunnel.

Say: Let's pretend our line is the crowd of people listening to Jesus. We have to go through the crowd to get close to Jesus.

Begin with the child at the back of the line.

Say: (*Child's name*), come to see Jesus. (*Have the child crawl through the tunnel of legs to the front of the line. Have the child stand up and take his or her place at the front of the line.*) (*Child's name*), Jesus loves you!

Continue until everyone has crawled through the tunnel.

© 1997 Abingdon Press.

Game 2

Supplies: scarf

Wave and Wiggle

Say: Let's play a game with this scarf. Each of you will have a turn holding the scarf. When you have the scarf, listen carefully and move as I tell you to move. Then give the scarf to the friend standing next to you.

Choose four children to stand up in front

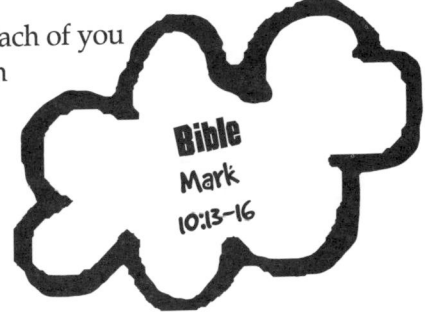

**Bible
Mark
10:13-16**

of the other children. Give the first child the scarf. Say the first two lines of the rhyme below. Encourage the child to move as directed. Give the scarf to the next child. Say the next two lines. Have the next child move as directed. Play until all four children have had a turn.

Choose four more children to stand up. Repeat the rhyme until everyone has a turn moving with the scarf.

> This little child waved the scarf down low,
> Jumped up once, then touched his (her) toes.
> This little child waved the scarf in the air,
> Turned around, then climbed up stairs.
> This little child waved the scarf all around,
> Hopped on one foot, then touched the ground.
> This little child waved the scarf up high,
> Touched the floor, then touched the sky.
> These little children were happy, you see,
> Happy that Jesus loves you and me!

© 1997 Abingdon Press.

Game 3

Supplies: stop sign (see page 79)

Stop!

Photocopy the stop sign (see page 79). Have the children go to one side of the room. Make sure the area between that space and the other side of the room is clear of any obstacles.

Say: Today we're talking about how Jesus loved the children. Mothers and fathers wanted to bring their children to see Jesus. Some of Jesus' friends did not think Jesus had time for children. But Jesus told his friends to "Let the little children come to me." Let's pretend we are little children going to see Jesus. I will tell you how to come to Jesus. (*Show the children the stop sign.*) When you see the stop sign and hear me say, "Stop!" freeze right where you are.

Give the children the first direction and have them move across the room. After a few seconds hold up the stop sign and shout "Stop!" Have the children freeze wherever they are.

> Hop, little children, hop to see Jesus.
> March, little children, march to see Jesus.
> Tiptoe, little children, tiptoe to see Jesus.
> Crawl, little children, crawl to see Jesus.

© 1997 Abingdon Press.

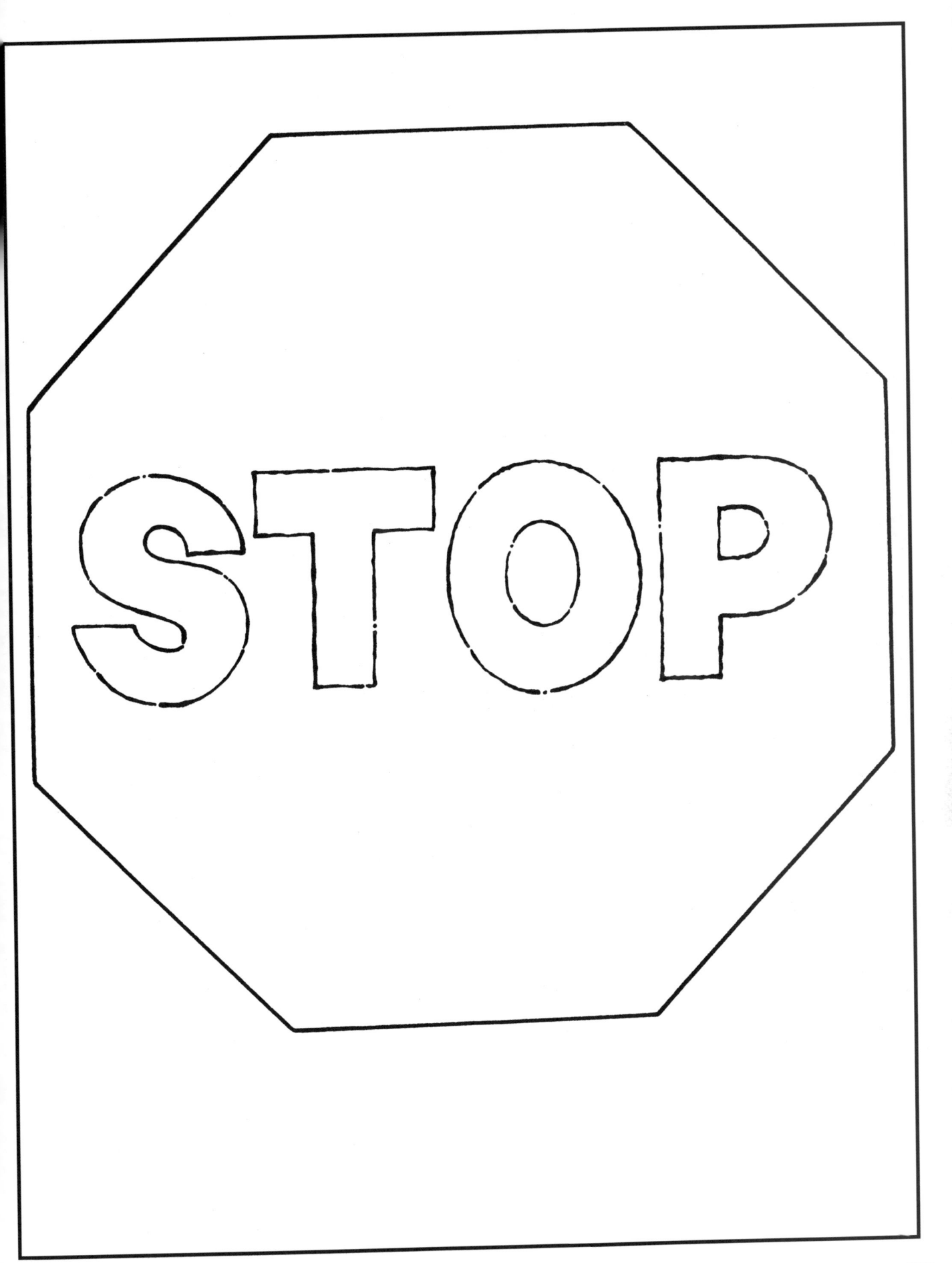
STOP

Jesus' Birth

Game 1

Follow the Leader

Have the children stand in an open area of the room.

Say: People all over the world celebrate Jesus' birthday. Let's play a game the children play in a country called Vietnam. To play this game, do what I do and say what I say.

Say: This is the way an elephant goes. (*Move like an elephant.*) Very good. Now let's pretend to be the animals that were at the stable when baby Jesus was born. This is the way a donkey goes. (*Move like a donkey.*) This is the way a sheep goes. (*Move like a sheep.*) This is the way a dove goes. (*Move like a bird.*) This is the way a cow goes. (*Move like a cow.*)

© 1998 Abingdon Press.

Game 2

Praise Ways

Have the children move to an open area of the room.

Say: People all over the world praise God for Jesus. Let's play a game like children play in a country called Kenya and in a country called the United States. Let's praise God for Jesus as we play.

Sing the following words to the tune of "This Is the Way." Lead the children in the suggested motions.

This is the way we go to the Temple,
(*March in place.*)
Go to the Temple, go to the Temple.
This is the way we go to the Temple
And thank God for Jesus.
(*Clap hands and turn around.*)

Bible
Luke
2:1-7

This is the way we see the baby, (*Make glasses with hands.*)
See the baby, see the baby.
This is the way we see the baby
And thank God for Jesus. (*Clap hands and turn around.*)

This is the way we hold the baby, (*Pretend to rock baby.*)
Hold the baby, hold the baby.
This is the way we hold the baby
And thank God for Jesus. (*Clap hands and turn around.*)

This is the way we show our praise, (*Shake hands above head.*)
Show our praise, show our praise.
This is the way we show our praise
And thank God for Jesus. (*Clap hands and turn around.*)

© 1998 Abingdon Press.

Game 3

Supplies: baby doll

Ring Around the Baby

Have the children stand in a circle. Place a baby doll in the center of the circle.

Say: Simeon and Anna waited and waited for a special gift from God. Baby Jesus was that special gift. When Simeon and Anna saw baby Jesus, they praised God. Let's praise God for Jesus.

Sing the following words to the tune of "Ring Around the Rosie." Sing the song several times and change the word *ring* to other movement words (*tiptoe, skip, hop, march*).

Ring around the baby,
This very special baby.
Praise God for Jesus.
Now all fall down.

© 1998 Abingdon Press.

Jesus Grows

Game 1

Wonder Works

Lead the children in the following movement activity.

Jesus grew from a baby, (*Rock baby in your arms.*)
Just like me and you. (*Point to self; point to others.*)
And when he grew into a boy, (*Crouch down, then stand up tall.*)
I wonder what he could do? (*Put finger on the side of your head.*)

   I wonder if Jesus could . . . jump! Let's all jump.
   I wonder if Jesus could . . . run! Let's all run in place.
   I wonder if Jesus could . . . hop! Let's all hop on one foot.
   I wonder if Jesus could . . . sit! Let's all sit down.

© 1999 Abingdon Press.

Game 2

Supplies: two chairs, ribbon

Learning Limbo

Place two chairs opposite each other in an open area of the room. Tie a length of ribbon (about four feet) between the two chairs. Have the children sit down on the floor, facing the ribbon.

   Say: As Jesus grew, he learned about God. Let's think about what we have learned about God.

Give the children the following directions. Have the children move back and forth underneath the ribbon as suggested.

**Bible
Luke
2:40**

   Say: If you have learned that God loves you, crawl under the ribbon. (*Have all the children*

82

crawl under the ribbon.) If you have learned that God is always with you, slide under the ribbon. (*Have all the children slide on their stomachs under the ribbon.*) If you have learned that you can talk to God anytime or anywhere, roll under the ribbon. (*Have the children lie down on the floor and roll under the ribbon.*)

© 1999 Abingdon Press.

Game 3

Hoppy Talk

Have the children move to one side of the room. Instruct the children to crouch down near the floor.

Say: Jesus grew from a baby to a boy. If you are growing, stand up tall. (*Have the children stand up on their tiptoes and stretch their arms above their heads.*)

Have the children stand straight.

Say: As Jesus grew, he learned many things. He learned to walk. If you can walk, hop one time. (*Have the children hop once.*) He learned to talk. If you can talk, hop two times. (*Have the children hop twice.*) He learned to run. If you can run, hop three times. (*Have the children hop three times.*)

Have all the children crouch near the floor.

Say: Jesus grew from a baby to a boy. As he grew, he learned about God. If you are learning about God, stand up tall. (*Have the children stand up on their tiptoes and stretch their arms above their heads.*)

Have the children stand straight.

Say: We have learned many things about God. We know that God made the world. We know that God wants us to be kind to one another. We know that God loves us. If you know that God loves you, hop four times. (*Have the children hop four times.*)

© 1997 Abingdon Press.

The Messiah

Game

Tell the Truth

Have the children sit down.

Say: Listen carefully to what I say. If what I say is the truth, everyone stand up. If what I say is not the truth, everyone sit down.

Have the children respond to the true statements by standing up, and the false statements by sitting down.

A kitten says meow.
A turtle has long ears and a fluffy tail.
Jesus loves you.
A duck says bow wow, bow wow.
The stars shine in the sky at night.
Jesus tells us about God's love.
A lion says tweet tweet.
Jesus is the Messiah.

Let the children take turns saying: "Jesus is the Messiah."

© 1997 Abingdon Press.

Bible
Luke
3:15-16

Jesus Calls Fishermen

Game 1

Disciple Doings

Have the children stand in a circle.

Say: Followers of Jesus are loving and kind. I am going to name some things to do. If followers of Jesus do what I say, then you say, "We can follow Jesus." If followers of Jesus do not do what I say, be very quiet.

I can push ahead of other children in the line waiting for the swings.
I can put all the caps on the markers for my teacher.
I can hide from Johnny when he comes over and wants to play.
I can make a get-well card for a friend who is sick.
I can take someone else's turn.
I can put napkins on the table to help Mother.
I can throw my toys on the floor and not pick them up.
I can give Mom and Dad a big hug when they pick me up from day care.
I can tell Bobby that he's not my friend.
I can give some of my candy to Julie because she dropped hers in the dirt.

© 2000 Abingdon Press.

Game 2

Supplies: blanket or quilt

Bible—Times Play

Bible
Luke
5:1-11

Say: Some people in Bible times were fishermen. Peter fished all night and didn't catch any fish in his net, but the next day he caught lots of fish when he threw the net into the water where Jesus told him to. Pretend that you are fish swimming in the Sea of Galilee and I am Peter. This is my net. (*Show the children the blanket or quilt.*) When I throw it out on the floor and say, "Any fish tonight?" everyone swim away from the net. But if I say, "Any fish today?" everyone swim onto the net and fill it full.

Show the children how to hold their hands in front of them with palms together and to wave their hands back and forth like fish swimming as they walk around the room.

Walk around among the fish and occasionally throw the blanket or quilt out on the floor, keeping hold of one corner of it. Say, "Any fish tonight?" two or three times before saying, "Any fish today?" When all the children are on the blanket, make a big production of the net being so full of fish that you cannot move it.

© 2000 Abingdon Press.

Game 3

Bring a Friend

Have the children choose a friend and go to one side of the room. If you have an uneven number of children, let the children make a group of three.

Say: When we are followers of Jesus, it is fun to tell our friends about Jesus and to invite them to church. Let's bring our friends to see Jesus.

Sit on the opposite side of the room from the children. Give the children directions on how to move with their friends across the room to you.

Friend (*child's name*) and friend (*child's name*), hold hands and gallop to see Jesus.
Friend (*child's name*) and friend (*child's name*), hold hands and hop to see Jesus.
Friend (*child's name*) and friend (*child's name*), hold hands and tiptoe to see Jesus.
Friend (*child's name*) and friend (*child's name*), hold hands and walk backwards to see Jesus.
Friend (*child's name*) and friend (*child's name*), hold hands and take giant steps to see Jesus.
Friend (*child's name*) and friend (*child's name*), hold hands and take baby steps to see Jesus.

© 1998 Abingdon Press.

The Prodigal Son

Game

Supplies: pig nose (see page 88), scissors, crayons, glue or tape

This Little Piggy

Photocopy and cut out a pig nose (see page 88) for each child. Give each child a pig nose. Let the children decorate the noses with crayons. Have each child fold the nose on the dotted lines. Glue or tape the flaps together. Help each child glue or tape a headband strip to one side of the nose. Measure the strip around the child's head. Glue or tape the other end of the strip to the opposite side of the pig nose so the nose fits around the child's head.

Say: Jesus told about a father and son. The son made a mistake, but his father still loved him. The pigs have something to do with the mistake that the son made.

Encourage the children to wear their pig noses and to pretend to be pigs. Use the following suggestions to help the children move around the room.

> This little piggy said, "Oink, oink, oink."
> This little piggy rolled in the mud.
> This little piggy ran around the pigpen.
> This little piggy ate a big supper.
> This little piggy took a nap in the sun.

© 1998 Abingdon Press.

Bible
Luke 15:11-24

Permission granted to photocopy for local church use. © 1998 Abingdon Press.

The Ten Lepers

Game 1

Supplies: paper or posterboard, marker, glue, construction paper

Sign of the Times

Print the phrase, "Thank you, God," on a large piece of paper or posterboard. Show the children the poster. Read the words to the children.

Say: Today we're talking about ten men who asked Jesus for help. The ten men all had sore places on their skin that were red and would not heal. Jesus helped the men. He made their skin better. The ten men were happy, but only one man said thank you to Jesus and praised God.

Have the children decorate the poster. Let the children help you glue the poster onto construction paper. Show the children how to tear colored construction paper into small pieces. Let the children glue the pieces to make a border around the poster.

Say: Let's say thank you to God.

Have the children stand in an open area of the room. Hold the poster so that the children can see it. Use the suggestions below to have the children move. Each time you hold up the poster, have the children stop moving and say the words.

We have two feet. Move your feet. Hop, jump, tiptoe. Shake one foot. Shake the other foot. (*Hold up sign.*) Thank you, God, for feet.

We have two hands. Move your hands. Stretch your hands up high. Now touch the floor. Clap your hands. Shake one hand. Shake the other hand. (*Hold up sign.*) Thank you, God, for hands.

We have two knees. Touch your knees. Bend your knees. Shake one knee. Shake the other knee. (*Hold up sign.*) Thank you, God, for knees.

We have two hips. Put your hands on your hips. Wiggle your hips. (*Hold up sign.*) Thank you, God, for hips.

We have one body. We have a head. Touch your head. We have ten toes. Touch your toes. We have one mouth. Point to your mouth. Now wiggle your whole body. (*Hold up sign.*) Thank you, God, for bodies.

Bible
Luke 17:11-19

© 1998 Abingdon Press.

Game 2

Ten Hop!

Have the children move to an open area of the room.

Say: Today we're hearing about Jesus and ten men. The ten men all had sore places on their skin that were red and would not heal. Jesus helped the ten men. He made their skin better. The ten men were happy, but only one of the men thanked Jesus. Only one of the men praised God for the wonderful thing that God had done for him.

Say the first verse of the rhyme printed below. Have the children hop as you count one through ten. Say the second verse of the rhyme. Then have the children hop and shout the number one.

How many men came to Jesus?
How many men did he see?
How many men came to Jesus?
Count and hop with me.
1, 2, 3, 4, 5, 6, 7, 8, 9, 10.

How many men said thank you?
How many men did he see?
How many men said thank you?
Count and hop with me.
One!

© 1998 Abingdon Press.

Game 3

Comeback Kid

Have the children sit down with you on one side of the room.

Say: Jesus helped ten men, but only one of them came back to thank Jesus.

Choose one child to begin the game. Start counting to ten. While you are counting, have the child move across to the other side of the room. When you say the number ten, shout, "Come back and say thank you!" Have the child turn around and hurry back to you.

Say: Thank you, God, for (*child's name*).

Continue the game until every child has had a turn moving across the room.

© 1998 Abingdon Press.

Zacchaeus

Game 1

Jump Up

Have the children make a line in an open area of the room. Stand in front of the line. Hold your hand up high and off to your side. Have the children take turns jumping up to touch your hand. Hold your hand down low to begin. After each child has had a turn touching your hand, hold it higher and let the children try again. Keep raising your hand until it is out of the children's reach.

Say: Jesus met a man named Zacchaeus. Zacchaeus was very short. He was so short that sometimes he could not see over other people's heads. One day Jesus came to town. Zacchaeus wanted to see Jesus, but he was so short, he could not see over the crowds of people. Zacchaeus did something so he could see Jesus. Can you guess what Zacchaeus did?

Let the children guess what Zacchaeus did. Accept the children's answers. Do not tell them if their answers are right or wrong.

© 1998 Abingdon Press.

Bible
Luke
19:1-8

Game 2

Supplies: masking tape or chairs, sticker

Where's Zacchaeus?

Use masking tape to mark a large square on the floor. Or block off an area by making a square of chairs. Be sure there is a wide space for the children to go into the area without knocking over chairs.

Say: Today we're hearing about a man named Zacchaeus. One day Zacchaeus heard that Jesus was coming to town. Zacchaeus climbed a tree to see Jesus. Jesus saw Zacchaeus in the tree.

Have the children repeat the Bible verse, "Jesus said, 'Zacchaeus, hurry and come down; for I must stay at your house today'" (Luke 19:5, adapted).

Say: When Zacchaeus met Jesus, he changed. He gave back all the money he had taken from the people. He was happy to know that Jesus loved him.

Have the children move freely about the room. Move among the children and pretend to put a sticker on the back of each child. Actually put a sticker on one child's back.

Shout: Look! Jesus is coming!

Have all the children run and stand inside the square.

Say: Where's Zacchaeus?

Have the children look around to find the child wearing the sticker on his or her back. Have that child repeat the Bible verse.

Take the sticker off Zacchaeus's back and have the children start moving around the room again. Play the game until everyone has had an opportunity to be Zacchaeus and to repeat the Bible verse.

© 1998 Abingdon Press.

Jesus' Baptism

Game 1

Supplies: blue crepe paper

In and Out the River

Have the children stand in a circle. Give each child a streamer made from blue crepe paper. Have the children hold their streamers so that their hands touch the hands of the person next to them. Instruct the children to hold their arms up to make windows. The streamers will hang down to make the water of the river.

Say: Jesus grew from a baby to a boy to a man. When Jesus was a man, he was baptized in the river. Let's pretend our circle of streamers is the river.

Choose one child to begin. Have that child stand in the middle of the circle. Let the child go in and out through the other children's arms. Sing the song below to the tune of "In and Out the Windows."

Go in and out the river,
Go in and out the river,
Go in and out the river,
For Jesus is God's son.

Sing the song over again until the child has gone in and out around the entire circle. Continue playing the game until every child has a turn.

© 1997 Abingdon Press.

Bible
John
1:29-34

Game 2

Fly Away

Have the children sit down in a circle in an open area of the room.

Say: As Jesus was baptized, a dove flew down from the sky, and a voice spoke. Jesus knew that God loved him and that he was God's son. Let's take turns pretending to be the dove.

Choose one child to be the dove. Have the dove fly around the outside of the circle as you say the following rhyme. When you say, "Fly back home, (*child's name*)," have the child sit back down. Repeat the rhyme and let each child have a turn flying around the circle as the dove.

See the dove flying in the sky.
Flying, flying up so high.
Flying down from up above.
To tell us all about God's love.
Fly back home, (*child's name*).
God loves you.

© 1999 Abingdon Press.

Game 3

Supplies: blue crepe paper

Water Wiggles

Tear off three or four long strips of blue crepe paper. Twist the ends of the strips together so that each end can be held by one child. Choose children to hold opposite ends of the strips. Have the children wave the strips up and down with big arm movements.

Say: Let's pretend that the blue streamers are water in a river.

Let the children take turns running underneath the strips. Have the children take turns holding the strips. Repeat the game, letting the children crawl and pretend to swim under the strips.

Have the children holding the strips place the strips on the floor. Show the children how to make the strips wiggle back and forth. Let the children take turns jumping over the strips.

© 1997 Abingdon Press.

Mud in the Eye

Game 1

Color Hop

Say: Today we're hearing about Jesus and a man who was blind. Jesus helped the man. He made the man see. Now the man could see the green grass and the yellow bumblebees. The man told everyone the wonderful thing God had done for him.

Say: Let's use our eyes to look for colors. Listen to my rhymes. When I name a color, look to find something in our room that is that color. Hop around the room to whatever you found and touch the color.

Say the rhymes printed below for the children.

> Look around, what do you see?
> I see colors all around me.
> I see colors all around you.
> Now please hop to the color blue.
>
> Look around, what do you see?
> I see colors all around me.
> I see colors over my head.
> Now please hop to the color red.
>
> Look around, what do you see?
> I see colors all around me.
> I see colors 'round each fellow.
> Now please hop to the color yellow.
>
> Look around, what do you see?
> I see colors all around me.
> I see colors cool and clean.
> Now please hop to the color green.
>
> Look around, what do you see?
> I see colors all around me.
> Thank you, God, for eyes to see
> All the colors dancing 'round me.

© 1998 Abingdon Press.

Bible
John 9:1–7

Game 2

I Spy

Say: Jesus helped the man who could not see. We can help others. One way we can help others is by praying for them.

Describe a child. Let the other children guess the child you are describing. Have the child stand up. Encourage the other children to look at the child. Sing the song printed below to the tune of "London Bridge."

I spy someone Jesus loves,
Jesus loves, Jesus loves.
I spy someone Jesus loves.
Thank you, God, for (*child's name*).

Have the child sit back down. Describe and pray for every child.

© 1998 Abingdon Press.

Game 3

Noisy Nonsense

Say: Today we're talking about a man who could not see. He wanted Jesus to help him. One day he heard people talking about Jesus. He could not see Jesus, but he listened very carefully so he would hear when Jesus was coming by him. Let's play a listening game.

Choose a child to be the noisemaker. Have the other children cover their eyes with their hands. Have the noisemaker make an animal sound. Let the children guess what the animal is. Continue the game until each child has an opportunity to be the noisemaker.

Say: When the man who could not see heard Jesus passing by, he asked Jesus for help. Jesus was a friend to the man who could not see. He cared for the man and helped him see again.

© 1997 Abingdon Press.

Foot Washing

Game

Feet Fun

Have the children move to an open area of the room. Say the following dialogue and have the children do the motions with you.

Say: In Bible times people wore sandals without socks or went barefoot. When they walked on the dirt roads, their feet got dusty and dirty. Let's pretend that we are Bible-times people. Let's put on our sandals.

Have the children pretend to put sandals on their feet.

Say: Now let's take a walk. (*Walk in place.*) What a dusty road! My feet are already dirty. (*Hold up one foot; hold up the other foot.*) The road is hot. Let's hop on one foot. (*Hop on one foot.*) Now let's hop on the other foot. (*Hop on other foot.*)

Say: Whew, I'm tired. (*Wipe hand over brow.*) Let's sit down and rest.

Have the children sit down in a circle.

Say: Put your feet out in front of you. (*Stretch legs out in front of your body.*) Wiggle your toes. (*Wiggle toes.*) Stand up. (*Stand up.*) Stomp each foot once. (*Stomp each foot.*)

© 1999 Abingdon Press.

Bible
John
13:4-16

Pentecost

Game

Supplies: typing paper, children's scissors, tissue paper, paper punch, plastic two-liter soft drink bottle, drinking straws

Wind Whipper

Say: Today we're hearing about a time when the followers of Jesus felt a special wind from God and knew that God loved them. We can't see God's love, and we can't see the wind, but we can see what the wind does. Let's make a wind whipper for our room so that we can see what the wind does and can remember that God loves us.

Put out a sheet of typing paper cut into eighths, tissue paper in about the same size pieces, and children's scissors. Encourage the children to snip and snip the papers into tiny pieces. Use the paper punch to punch out small circles as well.

When you have a nice pile of tiny paper scraps, put them into a two-liter soft drink bottle. (Be sure that it is completely dry inside.)

Give each child a straw and invite the children to take turns blowing into the bottle with their straws so that the class can see the paper scraps whirl around.

© 2000 Abingdon Press.

Bible
Acts 2:1-4

Peter and John Heal the Man at the Gate

Game 1

Leaping Feet

Say: Today we're talking about a man who could not walk. Something happened that had the man jumping for joy.

Have the children move to an open area of the room.

Say: Let's pretend we have leaping feet. Let me see you jump around the room.

Give the children a few minutes to jump and leap around the room. Then say "Stop!"

Lead the children in the following motions. After they move as directed for a few minutes, say "Stop!" and have the children freeze where they are. Give the next direction and encourage the children to move.

Jump on one foot.
Jump on two feet.
Jump forward three times.
Jump backwards one time.
Jump as high as you can.
Jump one time and then sit down.

Say: Peter and John were friends of Jesus. They did something to help the man who could not walk that had the man jumping for joy.

© 1997 Abingdon Press.

Bible
Acts
3:1-10

Game 2

Shake a Leg

Have the children sit so that there is room to stretch and move without touching another child.

Say: Let's pretend we cannot move our legs or arms. Stretch out on the floor and be very still.

Pause for a few minutes.

Say: Now let's move each arm and leg.

Give other suggestions, such as:

Lift one arm high in the air.
Shake your hand.
Wiggle your fingers.
Lift your other arm high in the air.
Wiggle your fingers.
Shake both hands.
Put your arms down.
Lift one leg high in the air.
Wiggle your foot.
Lift your other leg high in the air.
Wiggle your foot.
Wiggle both feet.
Put your legs back down.

Have the children sit up.

Say: Listen carefully. I will call each one of you by name. When I call your name, stand up and jump up and down. Then sit down.

Call each child by name. Have the child stand up, jump up and down, and sit down.

Say: Peter and John were friends of Jesus. They did something to help a man who could not walk. After Peter and John helped the man, the man jumped for joy.

© 1997 Abingdon Press.

Dorcas

Game 1

Supplies: garments, scarfs, grocery-size paper bag

Guess What Dorcas Made

Put several garments and scarfs in a pile behind some furniture or in a closet or other space where one child can go and not be seen by the others.

Explain to the children that each of them can have a turn taking a bag to the pile and selecting one garment to put in the bag. Then he or she can come back and hold the bag but not show what is in it.

Say: Dorcas has made something for (*child's name*). How many think that it is a coat? Jump up and down. How many think that it is a dress? Clap your hands. How many think that it is a scarf? Stamp your feet. OK, (*child's name*), show us what Dorcas made you. Oh! it's a (*name item*). Let's all do this. (*Have the children pantomime the motions involved in putting on the garment.*)

© 2000 Abingdon Press.

Game 2

Supplies: Bible-times costume or adult-size shirt

Tunic Tiptoe

Show the children how to put on a Bible-times costume or an adult-size shirt.

Say: Dorcas was a follower of Jesus. She sewed robes and clothing for people in need. Dorcas knew that followers of Jesus shared with others. Let's pretend this costume (or shirt) is one of the robes Dorcas made.

Bible
Acts
9:36-41

Place the costume or shirt over a chair on one side of the room. Place another chair on the opposite side of the room. Have the children line up behind the chair with the costume or shirt. Choose a child to begin. Have the child put on the costume or shirt (unbuttoned), tiptoe to the chair across the room, and then tiptoe back to the line.

Have the child take off the costume or shirt and give it to the next child in line. Have the next child put on the costume or shirt and tiptoe to the chair and back to the line. Continue until each child has had a turn.

© 1997 Abingdon Press.

Game 3

In and Out

Say: Dorcas made clothes for people in need. When Dorcas sewed, she would have pushed a needle in and out of the cloth to stitch the clothes together. (*Pantomime pushing a needle in and out of a piece of cloth.*) Let's pretend that we are Dorcas's needle going in and out of the cloth.

Move the children to an open area of the room. Have the children stand side by side and hold hands. Spread the children out so that they are standing with their arms outstretched and held up while they hold hands.

Choose the child at the beginning of the line to begin. This child will be Dorcas's needle. Have the needle weave in and out underneath the children's hands. When the needle comes to the end of the line, have the needle join hands with the line. The child now at the beginning of the line becomes the next needle.

Practice until the children understand the movement. Sing the following verse to the tune of "The Farmer in the Dell." Have the needle move in and out of the other children. Continue until each child has a turn.

The needle goes in and out,
The needle goes in and out.
Sewing robes for those in need,
The needle goes in and out.

© 1997 Abingdon Press.

Peter and Cornelius

Game 1

Down the Street

Have the children sit in a circle on the floor.

Say: Today we're talking about Peter and Cornelius. Peter was a friend of Jesus. Cornelius was a Roman soldier. Most people did not like Roman soldiers, but God showed Peter that God loves everyone. Peter went to the soldier's house and told him about Jesus.

Choose a child to be Peter. Sing the song below to the tune of "This Is the Way." Have Peter gallop around the inside of the circle as you sing together.

Peter comes walking down the street,
Down the street, down the street.
Peter comes walking down the street
To tell everyone about Jesus.

Sing the second verse printed below and have Peter kneel down and knock on the floor in front of one child seated in the circle.

Peter comes knocking at your door,
At your door, at your door.
Peter comes knocking at your door
To tell everyone about Jesus.

Have Peter change places with the seated child. The new child becomes Peter, and the game starts over again. Continue playing until each child has had an opportunity to be Peter. Have the children sit down.

© 1999 Abingdon Press.

Bible
Acts
10:1-35

Game 2

Peter, Peter

Say: Peter was a friend of Jesus. Cornelius was a Roman soldier. Most people did not like Roman soldiers, but God showed Peter that God loves everyone. Peter went to the soldier's house and told him about Jesus.

Say the following poem for the children. Have the children move as directed.

Peter, Peter, stand up tall.
(*Have the children stand up.*)
Peter, Peter, God loves us all.

Peter, Peter, walk to town.
(*Have the children walk around the room.*)
Peter, Peter, sit back down.
(*Have the children sit down.*)

Soldier, Soldier, stand up tall.
(*Have the children stand up.*)
Soldier, Soldier, God loves us all.

Soldier, Soldier, march to town.
(*Have the children march around the room.*)
Soldier, Soldier, sit back down.
(*Have the children sit down.*)

Peter, Peter, stand up tall.
(*Have the children stand up.*)
Peter, Peter, God loves us all.

Peter, Peter, tiptoe to town.
(*Have the children tiptoe around the room.*)
Peter, Peter, sit back down.
(*Have the children sit down.*)

Soldier, Soldier, stand up tall.
(*Have the children stand up.*)
Soldier, Soldier, God loves us all.

Soldier, Soldier, hop to town.
(*Have the children hop around the room.*)
Soldier, Soldier, sit back down.
(*Have the children sit down.*)

© 1999 Abingdon Press.

Paul's Travels

Game

Travel With Paul

Say: Today we're talking about a man named Paul. Paul traveled to many places to tell others about Jesus. Sometimes Paul walked, and sometimes Paul traveled by boat. Let's pretend to travel with Paul.

Lead the children around your room using the following rhyme. Do the suggested motions as you move.

Let's walk to town, Paul, Paul, Paul, (*Walk around the room.*)
And tell about Jesus to all, all, all.

We can go by camel. (*Pretend to ride a camel.*)
We can go by horse. (*Pretend to ride a horse.*)
We can even go by boat, (*Pretend to row a boat.*)
Of course!

Let's hop to town with Paul, Paul, Paul, (*Hop around the room.*)
And tell about Jesus to all, all, all.

We can go by camel. (*Pretend to ride a camel.*)
We can go by horse. (*Pretend to ride a horse.*)
We can even go by boat, (*Pretend to row a boat.*)
Of course!

Let's march to town, Paul, Paul, Paul, (*March around the room.*)
And tell about Jesus to all, all, all.

We can go by camel. (*Pretend to ride a camel.*)
We can go by horse. (*Pretend to ride a horse.*)
We can even go by boat, (*Pretend to row a boat.*)
Of course!

Let's tiptoe to town with Paul, Paul, Paul, (*Tiptoe around the room.*)
And tell about Jesus to all, all, all.

We can go by camel. (*Pretend to ride a camel.*)
We can go by horse. (*Pretend to ride a horse.*)
We can even go by boat, (*Pretend to row a boat.*)
Of course!

Bible
Acts
15:36

© 1999 Abingdon Press.

Paul and Silas in Jail

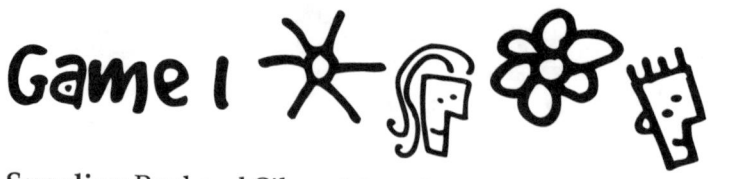

Game 1

Supplies: Paul and Silas picture (see page 107), tape

Stuck in Jail

Photocopy the Paul and Silas picture (see page 107) for each child. Tape the pictures to the floor in an open area of your room.

Say: When Paul and Silas were in jail, they were put in chains. The chains were fastened to the wall. Let's pretend our feet are chained to the floor. Place one foot on the picture. You cannot move your foot. (*Lead the children in different movements.*)

© 1999 Abingdon Press.

Game 2

Jailhouse Shake

Say: Paul and Silas were followers of Jesus. Some men did not like it when Paul and Silas told about Jesus. They had Paul and Silas put in jail. Let's pretend this is the jail where Paul and Silas told others about Jesus.

Have a child hold hands with you to make a bridge. Have the children stand in a line. Sing the song below (tune: "London Bridge"). Have the children march under the jail. On the last line, bring your arms down to catch a child.

Paul and Silas went to jail, went to jail, went to jail.
Paul and Silas went to jail; the door was locked up tight.

Sing the second verse. Rock your arms back and forth to make the jail shake. On the last line, release your hands and let the child go.

When the ground began to shake, began to shake, began to shake,
When the ground began to shake, the door was opened wide.

Have the child just caught change places with the child helping you make the jail. Play until each child has been caught in jail.

Bible: Acts 16:23-34

© 1999 Abingdon Press.

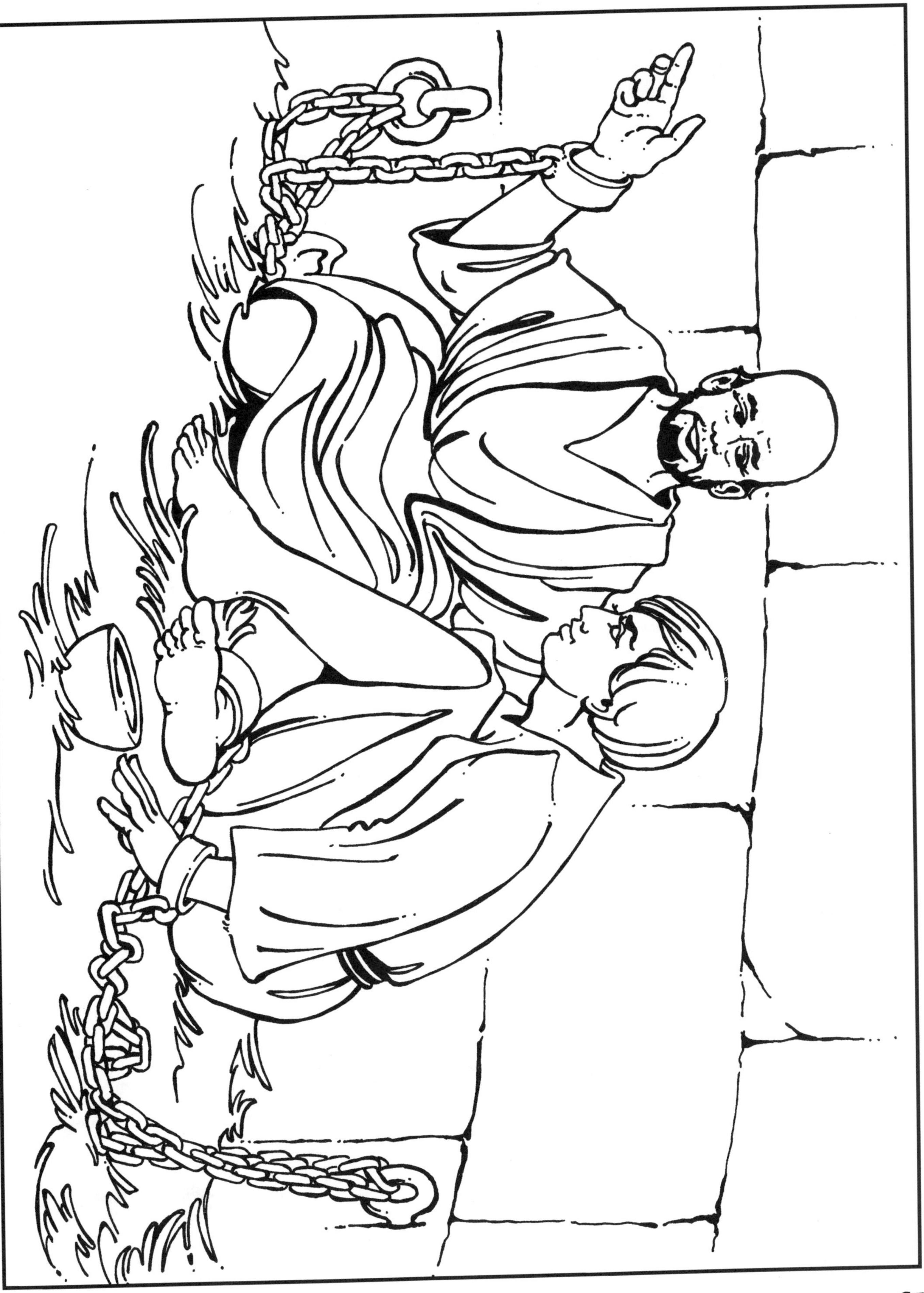

Paul's Letters

Game 1

Love in Action

Have the children move to an open area of the room. Say the statements printed below and do the suggested motions with the children.

Say: We show love when we smile at our friends. (*Point to mouth and smile.*) We show love when we are quiet so our baby sister can sleep. (*Tiptoe in place; put finger over lips.*) We show love when we pick up our toys. (*Pretend to pick up toys from the floor.*) We show love when we call our grandmothers on the telephone and say, "I love you!" (*Pretend to talk on phone.*)

© 1999 Abingdon Press.

Game 2

Supplies: cardboard, scissors, masking tape, crayons with paper removed, plain paper, yarn or ribbon

Lub Dub Rub

Cut hearts from cardboard. Use loops of masking tape to tape the hearts on the table. Place crayons (with paper removed) on the table.

Say: Hearts can help us remember about love.

Lightly tape plain paper over each heart. Let each child make a rubbing. Place a crayon on its side and rub it back and forth over the heart. Watch the pattern appear. Retape the paper in a different position. Have the child choose a different crayon. Have the child make rubbings until hearts cover the page.

Help the children roll the pictures like a scroll. Tie each scroll with a piece of yarn or ribbon. Write each child's name on the outside of the scroll.

Say: A man named Paul wrote letters to churches. Paul wrote that love never ends. He wanted people to know that Jesus will always love us.

Bible Galatians 5:22-23

© 1999 Abingdon Press.

Fruits of the Spirit

Game 1

Supplies: apple

Thank-You Pass

Have the children stand in a line, one behind the other.

Say: Gentleness is one of the fruits of the Spirit. When we are gentle, we are kind to one another. What are some ways we can be kind and gentle?

Help the children think of ways we can be kind and gentle, such as sharing toys, taking turns, helping each other, and saying "please" and "thank you."

Say: One way we can be kind to one another is to say, "Thank you." Let's pass the apple to each other. When you get the apple, say, "Thank you."

Give the first child in line an apple. Have the child gently pass the apple to the child behind him or her. Have that child take the apple and say, "Thank you."

Continue passing the apple down the line to the last child. Then have the child tiptoe to the front of the line and begin passing the apple again. Continue the game as long as the children show interest.

© 1999 Abingdon Press.

Bible
Ephesians
5:22-23

Game 2

Kindness Capers

Have the children move to an open area of the room.

Say: Kindness is one of the fruits of the Spirit. Today we're talking about Jesus and a man who could not move his hand. Jesus healed the hand so that it could move again. Jesus was kind to the man.

Talk with the children about ways we can be kind, such as taking turns, sharing toys, helping clean up, saying "please" and "thank you," and so forth.

Say: Listen to the things I say. If I say something that shows someone being kind, stretch your arms out and say, "Yes!" If I say something that shows someone not being kind, cross your arms over your chest and say, "No way!"

Susie saw her mother bringing in bags of groceries from the car. Susie hurried to the door and opened the door for her mother. Was Susie kind? (*Stretch out your arms and say, "Yes!"*)

Maggie wanted to play with the trucks. She ran over and grabbed a truck away from Pat. Was Maggie kind? (*Cross your arms over your chest and say, "No way!"*)

Jacob sat down at the table for snack time. When his teacher gave him a cookie, he smiled and said, "Thank you." Was Jacob kind? (*Stretch out your arms and say, "Yes!"*)

Brad was playing with the blocks. He was building a big tower. Matt came over and kicked Brad's tower down. Was Matt kind? (*Cross your arms over your chest and say, "No way!"*)

Carrie and Caleb brought cans of food to church to share with people who did not have money to buy food. Were Carrie and Caleb kind? (*Stretch out your arms and say, "Yes!"*)

© 1999 Abingdon Press.

Index by Bible Reference

Old Testament

Genesis
Genesis 1:14-18 (Sun, Moon, Stars) — page 8
Genesis 1:20-25 (God Made Animals) — page 9
Genesis 1:26-27 (In God's Image) — page 12
Genesis 6:14-19 (Noah) — page 13
Genesis 12:1-9; 18:1-15; 21:1-7 (Abraham and Sarah) — page 14
Genesis 28:10-21 (Jacob's Dream) — page 17
Genesis 37:12-28 (Joseph and His Brothers) — page 19

Exodus
Exodus 2:1-10 (Baby Moses) — page 21
Exodus 3:1-10 (The Burning Bush) — page 23
Exodus 7:1-2; 8:1-6, 20-24 (Let My People Go!) — page 25
Exodus 14:1-22 (The Red Sea) — page 27
Exodus 16:11-15 (In the Wilderness) — page 28
Exodus 20:1-17 (The Ten Commandments) — page 31

Joshua
Joshua 6:1-20 (Joshua and the Walls of Jericho) — page 33
Joshua 24:15 (Serve the Lord) — page 34

Ruth
Ruth 1–4 (Ruth and Naomi) — page 36

1 Samuel
1 Samuel 1:11-20 (Hannah) — page 40
1 Samuel 3:1-10 (Samuel's Calling) — page 42
1 Samuel 16:1-13 (Samuel Finds David) — page 43
1 Samuel 18:1-4 (David and Jonathan) — page 46

1 Kings
1 Kings 6:1-14; 8:62-63 (Solomon's Temple) — page 48

Esther
Esther 7:1-6; 8:16-17 (Esther) — page 51

Jeremiah
Jeremiah 1:4-10 (Jeremiah) — page 52
Jeremiah 18:1-6 (Potters) — page 53

Jonah
Jonah 1:1–3:3 (Jonah) — page 55

New Testament

Matthew
Matthew 2:1-11 (The Wise Men) — page 58
Matthew 5:3-12 (The Beatitudes) — page 61
Matthew 6:25-27 (The Least of These) — page 65
Matthew 18:10-14 (The Lost Sheep) — page 66
Matthew 18:21-22 (Forgive One Another) — page 68

Mark
Mark 3:1-5 (The Withered Hand) — page 70
Mark 6:7-13 (Two by Two) — page 74
Mark 10:13-16 (Jesus and the Children) — page 77

Luke
Luke 2:1-7 (Jesus' Birth) — 80
Luke 2:40 (Jesus Grows) — 82
Luke 3:15-16 (The Messiah) — page 84
Luke 5:1-11 (Jesus Calls Fishermen) — page 85
Luke 15:11-24 (The Prodigal Son) — page 87
Luke 17:11-19 (The Ten Lepers) — page 89
Luke 19:1-8 (Zacchaeus) — page 91

John
John 1:29-34 (Jesus' Baptism) — page 93
John 9:1-7 (Mud in the Eye) — page 95
John 13:4-16 (Foot Washing) — page 97

Acts
Acts 2:1-4 (Pentecost) — page 98
Acts 3:1-10 (Peter and John Heal the Man at the Gate) — page 99
Acts 9:36-41 (Dorcas) — page 101
Acts 10:1-35 (Peter and Cornelius) — page 103
Acts 15:36 (Paul's Travels) — page 105
Acts 16:23-34 (Paul and Silas in Jail) — page 106

Galatians
Galatians 5:22-23 (Paul's Letters) — page 108

Ephesians
Ephesians 5:22-23 (Fruits of the Spirit) — page 109

Index by Subject

Abraham and Sarah — page 14
Beatitudes, The — page 61
Creation: Animals — page 9
Creation: People — page 12
Creation: Sun, Moon, Stars — page 8
David and Jonathan — page 46
Dorcas — page 101
Esther — page 51
Foot Washing — page 97
Forgive One Another — page 68
Fruits of the Spirit — page 109
Hannah — page 40
Jacob's Dream — page 17
Jeremiah — page 52
Jesus and the Children — page 77
Jesus' Baptism — page 93
Jesus' Birth — 80
Jesus Calls Fishermen — page 85
Jesus Grows — 82
Jesus Heals (Mud in the Eye) — page 95
Jonah — page 55
Joseph and His Brothers — page 19
Joshua and the Walls of Jericho — page 33
Least of These, The — page 65
Lost Sheep, The — page 66
Messiah, The — page 84
Moses as a Baby — page 21

Moses, The Burning Bush — page 23
Moses, In the Wilderness — page 28
Moses, Let My People Go! — page 25
Moses, The Red Sea — page 27
Moses, The Ten Commandments — page 31
Noah — page 13
Paul and Silas in Jail — page 106
Paul's Letters — page 108
Paul's Travels — page 105
Pentecost — page 98
Peter and Cornelius — page 103
Peter and John Heal the Man at the Gate — page 99
Potters — page 53
Prodigal Son, The — page 87
Ruth and Naomi — page 36
Samuel Finds David — page 43
Samuel's Calling — page 42
Serve the Lord — page 34
Solomon's Temple — page 48
Ten Lepers, The — page 89
Two by Two — page 74
Wise Men, The — page 58
Withered Hand, The — page 70
Zacchaeus — page 91